PMLA ACT BAIL MATTERS- SUPREME COURT'S LEADING CASE LAWS

CASE NOTES- FACTS- FINDINGS OF APEX COURT JUDGES & CITATIONS

JAYPRAKASH BANSILAL SOMANI

Dedicated

To

All the Past & Present Judges of the Supreme Court of India.

Salute to their wisdom.

Salute to their interpretation of Law.

Salute to their elaborative judgement writing.

ೲ

ೲ

Contents

Contents

Preface

Dear Learned Advocates of the Special Courts, Session Courts, High Courts, Supreme Court & Individuals,

I am very delighted to provide you a book on 'PMLA ACT BAIL MATTERS'-Supreme Court of India Leading Case Laws.

In this book you will get...

1. Name of the Case i. e. Cause title

2. Relevant Sections discussed in the case

3. Hon'ble Judges/Coram of the case

4. Number of PDF Pages in Original Judgement of the case

5. All available Citations of the case

6. Case Note with appeal allowed/ dismissed or disposed off

7. Facts of the case

8. Hon'ble Apex Court's findings, while dismissing/allowing or disposing the appeal

9. Ratio Decidendi if any.

My special thanks to Manupatra, because of their web portal I can compile this book in well manner. I am also thankful to Notion Press to support me to publish & market this book throughout the Country. Thanks to my Juniors, Advocate Colleagues & Insolvency Professional Colleagues to support me in this venture.

Miss Shruti Kriti has helped me a lot to compile this book.

I hope this book will add some value addition in the wealth of your legal knowledge. Your positive feedbacks will boost me to compile/ write further books & negative feedbacks will improve my skills. Kindly send your valuable feedbacks by email.

Thanks with Regards,

Jayprakash B. Somani

Advocate, Supreme Court of India

Email: jaysomani64@gmail.com

Web Site: www.jayprakashsomani.com

Call: 9322188701, 8459194576

ACKNOWLEDGEMENTS

Printed & Published by
Notion Press
No. 8, 3rd Cross Street,
CIT Colony, Mylapore,
Chennai, Tamil Nadu- 600004

೮

Managed by
Jayprakash Somani Advocates & Solicitors
Law Firm for Supreme Court of India
Delhi Office
B- 851, 1st Floor, Shivaji Marg, New Ashok Nagar, Delhi 110096.
Call: 9322188701, 8459194576
Supreme Court Chamber
312, 3rd Floor, M. C. Setalvad Block, In front of 'D' Gate, Bhagwan Das
Road, Supreme Court of India, New Delhi 110001
Contact: 8459194576, 9811011747
www.jayprakashsomani.com

೮

Books are available online in India
1. Notion Press:https://notionpress.com/author/jayprakash_somani
2. Amazon:https://www.amazon.in/s?k=jayprakash+somani
3. Flipkart:https://www.flipkart.com/search?q=Jayprakash%20Somani
Books are available online at International Market
4.   Amazon   International: https://www.amazon.com/s?k=jayprakash+somani
5.   Amazon   United   Kingdom: https://www.amazon.co.uk/s?k=jayprakash+somani
6. E-Books/Kindle edition at National & International Level: https://www.amazon.in/s?k=jaypraksh+somani

೮

I

P. Chidambaram Vs. Directorate of Enforcement, 2019

Hon'ble Judges/Coram: R. Banumathi, A.S. Bopanna and Hrishikesh Roy, JJ.

Act/ Sections: Section 439 of Code of Criminal Procedure, 1973; Section 3 and 4 of Prevention of Money Laundering Act, 2002

No. of pages of the Original Judgement: 12

Citation: AIR2020SC1699, (2020)13SCC791, MANU/SC/1670/2019

Case Notes: Criminal - Bail - Grant of - Section 439 of Code of Criminal Procedure, 1973; Section 3 and 4 of Prevention of Money Laundering Act, 2002 - Respondent registered case against Appellant under Section 3 of Act punishable under Section 4 of Act - Subsequently, Appellant was arrested and Trial Court remanded Appellant to custody of Respondent - After his arrest, Appellant moved regular bail application before High Court under Section 439 of Code - High Court concluded that prima facie, allegations were serious in nature and Appellant had played key and active role in present case - High Court dismissed bail application filed by Appellant - Hence, present appeal- Whether Appellant is entitled to bail.

Facts: The Respondent Directorate of Enforcement registered a case against Appellant-Accused under Section 3 of Prevention of Money Laundering Act, 2002 punishable under Section 4 of the said Act with allegations that one company sought approval of Foreign Investment Promotion Board for permission to issue by way of preferential allotment, certain equity and convertible, non-cumulative, redeemable preference shares for engaging in the business of creating, operating, managing and broadcasting of bouquet of television channels. This proposal was favourably considered and approved by the Appellant. Subsequently, the Appellant was arrested and the Trial Court remanded the Appellant to the custody of the Respondent. After his arrest, the Appellant moved a regular bail application before the High Court under Section 439 of Code of Criminal Procedure, 1973. The High Court concluded that prima facie, allegations are serious in nature and the Appellant had played key and active role in the present case. On the basis of these observations, the High Court dismissed the bail application.

Hon'ble Apex Court Held, while allowing the appeal: This Court was not very much inclined to open the sealed cover although the materials in sealed cover was received from the Respondent. However, since the Single Judge of the High Court had perused the documents in sealed cover and arrived at certain conclusion and since that order was under challenge, it had become imperative to also open the sealed cover and peruse the contents so as to satisfy ourselves to that extent. On perusal this Court had taken note that the statements of persons concerned had been recorded and the details collected have been collated. The recording of statements and the collation of material was in the nature of allegation against one of the Co-Accused for opening shell companies and also purchasing benami properties in the name of relatives at various places in different countries. Except for recording the same, this court did not wish to advert to the documents any further since ultimately, these were allegations which would have to be established in the trial wherein the Accused/Co-Accused would have the opportunity of putting forth their case, if any, and an ultimate conclusion would be reached. Hence, the finding recorded by the Judge of the High Court based on the material in sealed cover was not justified.

(ii) While considering the bail application of the Appellant what was to be taken note was that, at a stage when the Appellant was before this Court in an application seeking for interim protection/anticipatory bail, this Court while considering the matter in Criminal Appeal had in that regard held that in a matter of present nature wherein grave economic offence was alleged, custodial interrogation as contended would be necessary and, in that circumstance, the anticipatory bail was rejected. Subsequently the Appellant had been taken into custody and had been interrogated and for the said purpose the Appellant was available in custody in this case. It was, however, contended on behalf of the Respondent that the witnesses will have to be confronted and as such custody was required for that purpose. The Appellant had not been named as one of the Accused in the ECIR but the allegation while being made against the Co-Accused it was indicated the Appellant who was the finance minister at that point, had aided the illegal transactions since one of the Co-Accused was the son of the Appellant. In this context even if the statements on record and materials gathered were taken note, the complicity of the Appellant would have to be established in the trial and if convicted, the Appellant would undergo sentence. For the present, as taken note the anticipatory bail had been declined earlier and the Appellant was available for custodial interrogation for more than forty-five days. In addition to the custodial interrogation if further investigation was to be made, the Appellant would be bound to participate in such investigation as is required by the Respondent. Further it was noticed that one of the Co-Accused had been granted bail by the High Court while the other Co-Accused was enjoying interim protection from arrest. The Appellant was aged about seventy-four years and as noted by the High Court itself in its order, the Appellant had already suffered two bouts of illness during incarceration and was put on antibiotics and had been advised to take steroids of maximum strength. In that circumstance, the availability of the Appellant for further investigation, interrogation and facing trial was not jeopardized and he was already held to be not a flight risk and there was no possibility of tampering the evidence or influencing/intimidating the witnesses. Taking these and all other facts and circumstances including the duration of custody into consideration the Appellant was entitled to be granted bail. It was made clear that the observations contained touching upon the merits either in the order of the High Court or in this order shall not be construed as an opinion expressed on merits and all contentions were left open to be considered during the course of trial.

II

Gautam Kundu Vs Manoj Kumar, Govt. of India, 2015

Hon'ble Judges/Coram: Pinaki Chandra Ghose and R.K. Agrawal, JJ.

Act/ Sections: Section 11(C)(3) of SEBI Act, Section 24 of SEBI Act, Section 8(1) of PMLA, Under Section 4 of PMLA, Section 439 of Code of Criminal Procedure, Section 45 of the PMLA

No.of pages of the Original Judgment: 13

Citation: AIR2016SC106, (2015)16SCC1, MANU/SC/1453/2015

Case Note: Criminal - Refusal to grant bail - Appellant - Chairman of Rose Valley - Public Company incorporated and registered under Companies Act, 1956 - Certain non-convertible debentures issued by Rose valley - 'Private placement method' - No advertisements issued to public - Issued to employees, their friends and associates - Fulfilled formalities of private placement - Appellant collected money - Issue of debentures from time to time - Letter issued by SEBI - Informed Appellant about offences alleged to have committed by it - Appeal filed before SAT allowed - Held - Appellant Company had repaid all money collected from investors - Further held - No grounds for violation of Section 11(C)(3) of SEBI Act - Report filed by Respondent - Alleged commission of offence under Section 24 of SEBI Act - Proceedings challenged in High Court - Pending for hearing - SEBI directed Appellant to refund money to customers of Ashirbad scheme - Order challenged before SAT - Show Cause Notice under Section 8(1) of PMLA

"

served - Appellant filed writ petition before High Court - Challenged notice - Dismissed – Appeal to Division Bench - Dismissed - Division Bench directed Appellant to appear before Adjudicating Authority - Authority to pass a reasoned order - Complaint filed by Respondent in Court of learned Chief Judge, City Sessions Court - Under Section 4 of PMLA - Appellant arrested on suspicion of commission of offence punishable under provisions of PMLA - Detained in custody since - Appellant - Granted bail of father's death - Surrendered later - Filed a fresh bail application - Section 439 of Code of Criminal Procedure - High Court rejected said application - Present Appeal -Whether the provisions of Section 45 of the PMLA are binding on the High Court while considering the application for bail Under Section 439 of the Code of Criminal Procedure - Whether the High Court has exercised its discretion under Section 439 of Code of Criminal Procedure, 1973 capriciously or arbitrarily by refusing bail to the Appellant

Facts: The Appellant is the Chairman of Rose Valley Real Estate Construction Ltd. (Rose Valley), a public company incorporated in 1999 and registered under the Companies Act, 1956. Certain non-convertible debentures were issued by the Rose Valley by 'private placement method.' No advertisements etc. were issued to the public. The said debentures were issued to the employees of the Company and to their friends and associates after fulfilling the formalities for private placement of debentures. Thus, the Appellant collected money by issuing secured debentures by way of private placement in compliance with the guidelines issued by the Securities and Exchange Board of India (SEBI) from time to time.

In 2013, the Adjudicating Officer, SEBI, passed an order imposing a penalty of Rs. 1 crore upon the Rose Valley for violation of the provisions of Sections 11(C) of the Securities and Exchange Board of India Act, 1992 (the SEBI Act) which was reduced to Rs. 10 lakhs by the Securities Appellate Tribunal. A letter was issued by SEBI to the Appellant informing about the offences alleged to have been committed by it under the Companies Act, SEBI Act & Regulations, and Section 405 of the Indian Penal Code, 1860. The appeal filed by the Appellant before the Securities Appellate Tribunal was allowed holding that the Appellant Company has repaid all the money collected from the investors. It was further held by the Securities Appellate Tribunal that there are no grounds for violation of Section 11(C)(3) of the SEBI Act.

On basis of letter issued by SEBI, the Respondent filed a report, alleging commission of offence by the Rose Valley and its officers, punishable Under

Section 24 of the SEBI Act. A complaint was filed by the Respondent authorities, alleging that the Rose Valley transferred the money raised by issue of debentures from the account of one company to that of another company. It is also alleged that the money collected by issuing the debentures for the purpose of one business has been invested in some other business. The proceedings Under Section 24 of the SEBI Act has been challenged in the High Court by way of revision which is pending for hearing and further proceeding of the complaint case, has been stayed by the High Court. The High Court also directed the Respondent not to take any coercive measure against the Appellant.

Vide its order, SEBI directed Appellant Rose Valley to refund the money to the customers of Ashirbad scheme. This order was challenged before the Securities Appellate Tribunal by way of appeal. A Show Cause Notice Under Section 8(1) of the Prevention of Money Laundering Act, 2002 (PMLA) was served upon Rose Valley and its officials. Rose Valley filed a writ petition before the High Court challenging the said Show Cause Notice. The said writ petition was dismissed by the learned Single Judge of the High Court. Thereafter, the matter was taken in appeal before the Division Bench. The Division Bench dismissed the said appeal and directed the Appellant Rose Valley to appear before the Adjudicating Authority Under Section 8 of the PMLA and directed the Adjudicating Authority to decide the preliminary objections as may be raised by the Rose Valley, including the applicability of the PMLA as also the validity of the search and seizure against Rose Valley. It was further directed that the Adjudicating Authority should pass a reasoned order in the matter and communicate the same to the Appellant.

A complaint was filed by the Respondent in the Court of learned Chief Judge, City Sessions Court against the Appellant Under Section 4 of PMLA, though no offence is made out against the Appellant Under Section 3 of the PMLA. Despite having fully cooperated with the investigation, the Appellant was arrested on suspicion of having committed an offence punishable under the provisions of the PMLA and is detained in custody since then.

While the Appellant was in custody, his father expired upon which he moved an application before the High Court for interim bail to perform the rituals for his deceased father. The High Court directed release of the Appellant on provisional bail for two weeks on the conditions mentioned in the said order. On completion of the period of provisional bail, the Appellant duly surrendered before the Court of learned Chief Judge, City Sessions

Court.

In July 2015, Appellant filed a fresh bail application under Section 439 of the Code of Criminal Procedure before the High Court. Vide impugned judgment and order the High Court has rejected the said application of the Appellant holding that no order has yet been passed by any competent Court of law that no offence is made out against the Appellant Under Section 24 of the SEBI Act. A criminal revision praying for quashing of the proceedings initiated against the Appellant Under Section 24 of the SEBI Act is still pending for decision before the High Court. Aggrieved by the rejection of the bail application filed Under Section 439 of the Code of Criminal Procedure, the Appellant has approached this Court through this appeal by special leave.

Hon'ble Apex Court Held, while dismissing the appeal: 1. There is no doubt that PMLA deals with the offence of money laundering and the Parliament has enacted this law as per commitment of the country to the United Nations General Assembly. PMLA is a special statute enacted by the Parliament for dealing with money laundering. Section 5 of the Code of Criminal Procedure, 1973 clearly lays down that the provisions of the Code of Criminal Procedure will not affect any special statute or any local law. In other words, the provisions of any special statute will prevail over the general provisions of the Code of Criminal Procedure in case of any conflict.

2. The conditions specified Under Section 45 of the PMLA are mandatory and needs to be complied with which is further strengthened by the provisions of Section 65 and also Section 71 of the PMLA. Section 65 requires that the provisions of Code of Criminal Procedure shall apply in so far as they are not inconsistent with the provisions of this Act and Section 71 provides that the provisions of the PMLA shall have overriding effect notwithstanding anything inconsistent therewith contained in any other law for the time being in force. PMLA has an overriding effect and the provisions of Code of Criminal Procedure would apply only if they are not inconsistent with the provisions of this Act. Therefore, the conditions enumerated in Section 45 of PMLA will have to be complied with even in respect of an application for bail made Under Section 439 of Code of Criminal Procedure That coupled with the provisions of Section 24 provides that unless the contrary is proved, the Authority or the Court shall presume that proceeds of crime are involved in money laundering and the burden to

prove that the proceeds of crime are not involved, lies on the Appellant.

3. The Court refrained itself from deciding the questions tried to be raised since it is nothing but a bail application. The Court did not forget that this case is relating to "Money Laundering" which it feels is a serious threat to the national economy and national interest. The Court could not brush aside the fact that the schemes have been prepared in a calculative manner with a deliberative design and motive of personal gain, regardless of the consequence to the members of the society.

4. With regard to the questions raised by learned senior Counsel appearing on behalf of the Appellant, at this stage, the Court did not think that it should answer or deal with the same in view of the fact that the matter is pending before a Division Bench of the High Court in writ jurisdiction. Hence, any observation or remarks made by the Court may cause prejudice to the case of both the sides. Therefore, the Court felt that it would be proper for it only to deal with the matter concerning bail.

5. The Court noted that admittedly the complaint is filed against the Appellant on the allegations of committing the offence punishable Under Section 4 of the PMLA. The contention raised on behalf of the Appellant that no offence Under Section 24 of the SEBI Act is made out against the Appellant, which is a scheduled offence under the PMLA, needs to be considered from the materials collected during the investigation by the Respondents. There is no order as yet passed by a competent court of law, holding that no offence is made out against the Appellant Under Section 24 of the SEBI Act and it would be noteworthy that a criminal revision praying for quashing the proceedings initiated against the Appellant Under Section 24 of SEBI Act is still pending for hearing before the High Court.

6. The Court further noted that Section 45 of the PMLA will have overriding effect on the general provisions of the Code of Criminal Procedure in case of conflict between them. Section 45 of the PMLA imposes two conditions for grant of bail, specified under the said Act. The Court has not missed the proviso to Section 45 of the said Act which indicates that the legislature has carved out an exception for grant of bail by a Special Court when any person is under the age of 16 years or is a woman or is a sick or infirm. Therefore, there is no doubt that the conditions laid down Under Section 45A of the PMLA, would bind the High Court as the provisions of special law having overriding effect on the provisions of Section 439 of the Code of Criminal Procedure for grant of bail to any person accused of committing offence punishable Under Section 4 of the PMLA, even when the

application for bail is considered Under Section 439 of the Code of Criminal Procedure.

7. The Court could not brush aside the fact that the Appellant floated as many as 27 companies to allure the investors to invest in their different companies on a promise of high returns and funds were collected from the public at large which were subsequently laundered in associated companies of Rose Valley Group and were used for purchasing moveable and immoveable properties

8. The Court did not intend to further state the other facts excepting the fact that admittedly the complaint was filed against the Appellant on the allegation of committing offence punishable Under Section 4 of the PMLA. The contention made on behalf of the Appellant that no offence Under Section 24 of the SEBI Act is made out against the Appellant, which is a scheduled offence under the PMLA, needs to be considered from the material collected during the investigation and further to be considered by the competent court of law. The Court did not intend to express itself at this stage with regard to the same as it may cause prejudice the case of the parties in other proceedings. The Court was sure that it is not expected at this stage that the guilt of the accused has to be established beyond reasonable Doubt through evidences.

9. The Court further noted that the High Court at the time of refusing the bail application, duly considered this fact and further considered the statement of the Assistant General Manager of RBI, Kolkata, seizure list, statements of directors of Rose Valley, statements of officer bearers of Rose Valley, statements of debenture trustees of Rose Valley, statements of debenture holders of Rose Valley, statements of AGM of Accounts of Rose Valley and statements of Regional Managers of Rose Valley for formation of opinion whether the Appellant is involved in the offence of money laundering.

10. In these circumstances, the Court did not find that the High Court exercised its discretion capriciously or arbitrarily in the facts and circumstances of this case. It further noted that the High Court had called for all the relevant papers and duly taken note of that and thereafter after satisfying its conscience, refused the bail. Therefore, the Court did not find that the High Court had committed any wrong in refusing bail in the given circumstances. Accordingly, Court did not find any reason to interfere with the impugned order so passed by the High Court and the bail, as prayed

before it, challenging the said order was refused. Consequently, the appeal is dismissed.

III

Union of India (UOI) Vs. Hassan Ali Khan and Ors., 2011

Hon'ble Judges/Coram: Altamas Kabir and S.S. Nijjar, JJ.

Act/ Sections: Code of Criminal Procedure, 1973 - Section 439--Prevention of Money Laundering Act, 2002--Section 4

No. of pages of the original Judgement: 08

Citation: [2011]11SCR778, MANU/SC/1144/2011

Case Note: Code of Criminal Procedure, 1973 - Section 439--Prevention of Money Laundering Act, 2002--Section 4--Bail--Cancellation-Offence under Section 4

Facts: establishing that if respondent No. 1 released on bail--He may abscond--Impugned order of High Court granting bail to said respondent set aside--Bail cancelled. It is true that at present, there is only a nebulous link between the huge sums of money handled by the respondent No. 1 and any arms deal or intended arms deals, there is no attempt on the part of the respondent No. 1 to disclose the source of the large sums of money handled by him. There is no denying the fact that allegations have been made that the said monies were the proceeds of crime and by depositing the same in his bank accounts, the respondent No. 1 had attempted to project the same as untainted money. The said allegations may not ultimately be established, but having been made, the burden of proof that the said monies were not the proceeds of crime and were not, therefore, tainted shifted to the respondent

No. 1 under Section 24 of the Prevention of Money Laundering Act. 2002 (P.M.L. Act). The High Court having proceeded on the basis that the attempt made by the prosecution to link up the acquisition by the respondent No. 1 of different Passports with the operation of the foreign bank accounts by the said respondent, was not believable, failed to focus on the other parts of the prosecution case. It is true that having a foreign bank account and also having sizeable amounts of money deposited therein does not ipso facto indicate the commission of an offence under the P.M.L. Act, 2002. However, when there are other surrounding circumstances which reveal that there were doubts about the origin of the accounts and the monies deposited therein, the same principles would not apply. The deposit of US$ 700,000 in the Barclays Bank account of the respondent No. 1 has not been denied. On the other hand, the allegation is that the said amount was the proceeds of the sale of diamond Jewellery which is alleged to have been stolen from the collection of the Nizam of Hyderabad. In fact, on behalf of the respondent No. 1. it has been submitted that in respect of the said deal, the respondent No. 1 had received by way of commission a sum of US$ 30.000 which he had spent in Dubai. The fact cannot be ignored that the total income of the respondent No. 1 for the assessment years 2001-02 to 2007-08 has been assessed at ' 110,412.68.85.303 by the Income Tax Department and in terms of Section 24 of the P.M.L. Act. the respondent No. 1 had not been able to establish that the same were neither the proceeds of crime nor untainted property. In addition to the above is the other factor involving the notarized document in which the name of Adnan Khashoggi figures. Lastly, the manner in which the respondent No. 1 had procured three different passports in his name, after his original passport was directed to be deposited, lends support to the apprehension that, if released on bail, the respondent No. 1 may abscond.

<h1 style="text-align:center">IV</h1>

Rohit Tandon Vs. The Enforcement Directorate,2017

Hon'ble Judges/Coram: Dipak Misra, C.J.I., A.M. Khanwilkar and D.Y. Chandrachud, JJ.

Act Sections:Sections 3, 4 and 45 of Prevention of Money Laundering Act, 2002

No. of pages of the original Judgement: 17

Citation: AIR2017SC5309, (2018)11SCC46, MANU/SC/1403/2017

Case Note: Criminal - Rejection of bail - Challenged thereto - Sections 3, 4 and 45 of Prevention of Money Laundering Act, 2002 - Appellant was arrested in connection with criminal case registered under Sections 3 and 4 of Act - Appellant first approached Additional Sessions Judge for releasing him on bail by way of application - Bail application came to be rejected - Appellant thereafter approached High Court by way of bail application and interlocutory application filed therein - High Court rejected prayer for bail vide impugned judgment - Hence, present appeal - Whether Appellant was entitled for enlargement on bail

Facts: The Appellant was arrested in connection with criminal case registered under Sections 3 and 4 of the Prevention of Money-Laundering Act, 2002. The Appellant first approached the Additional Sessions Judge for releasing him on bail by way of an application. The said bail application came to be rejected vide judgment by the said Court. The Appellant thereafter approached the High Court by way of bail application and an interlocutory application filed therein. The High Court independently considered the merits of the arguments but eventually rejected the prayer for bail vide impugned judgment. Hence, present appeal.

Hon'ble Apex Court Held, while dismissing the appeal: (i) The Appellant has not succeeded in persuading us about the inapplicability of the threshold stipulation under Section 45 of the Act. Present Court also noted the inexplicable silence or reluctance of the Appellant in disclosing the source from where such huge value of demonetized currency and also new currency has been acquired by him. The prosecution was relying on statements of many witnesses/accused already recorded, out of which few were considered by High Court. The same makes out a formidable case about the involvement of the Appellant in commission of a serious offence

of money-laundering. It was, therefore, not possible for to record satisfaction that there were reasonable grounds for believing that the Appellant was not guilty of such offence. Further, the Lower Courts have justly adverted to the antecedents of the Appellant for considering the prayer for bail and concluded that it was not possible to hold that the Appellant was not likely to commit any offence ascribable to the Act of 2002 while on bail. Since the threshold stipulation predicated in Section 45 has not been overcome, the question of considering the efficacy of other points urged by the Appellant to persuade the Court to favour the Appellant with the relief of regular bail would be of no avail.

(ii) The fact that no limit for deposit was specified, would not extricate the Appellant from explaining the source from where such huge amount has been acquired, possessed or used by him. The volume of demonetized currency recovered from the office and residential premises of the Appellant, including the bank drafts in favour of fictitious persons and also the new currency notes for huge amount, leave no manner of doubt that it was the outcome of some process or activity connected with the proceeds of crime projecting the property as untainted property. No explanation has been offered by the Appellant to dispel the legal presumption of the property being proceeds of crime. Similarly, the fact that the Appellant has made declaration in the Income Tax Returns and paid tax as per law does not extricate the Appellant from disclosing the source of its receipt. No provision in the taxation laws has been brought to notice which grants immunity to the Appellant from prosecution for an offence of money-laundering. In other words, the property derived or obtained by the Appellant was the result of criminal activity relating to a scheduled offence. The argument of the Appellant that there was no allegation in the charge-sheet filed in the scheduled offence case or in the prosecution complaint that the unaccounted cash deposited by the Appellant was the result of criminal activity, would not come to the aid of the Appellant. That would have to be negatived in light of the materials already on record. The possession of such huge quantum of demonetized currency and new currency, without disclosing the source from where it was received and the purpose for which it was received, the Appellant had failed to dispel the legal presumption that he was involved in money-laundering and the property was proceeds of crime.

V

Nikesh Tarachand Shah Vs. Union of India (UOI) and Ors., 2017

Hon'ble Judges/Coram: Rohinton Fali Nariman and Sanjay Kishan Kaul, JJ.

Act/ Sections: Section 45 of Prevention of Money Laundering Act, 2002 (Act) - Articles 14 and 21 of Constitution of India, constitutional validity of Section 45 of Act.

No. Of pages of the original Judgement: 27

Citation: AIR2017SC5500, (2018)11SCC1, MANU/SC/1480/2017

Case Note: Criminal - Grant of bail - Challenged therein - Section 45 of Prevention of Money Laundering Act, 2002 (Act) - Articles 14 and 21 of Constitution of India - Present appeal filed questioning constitutional validity of Section 45 of Act - Whether Section 45 of Act, arbitrary, discriminatory and violative of Appellant's fundamental

Facts: Present appeal was filed questioning constitutional validity of Section 45 of the Act, imposing two conditions for grant of bail. The conditions were that, public prosecutor must be given an opportunity to oppose any application for release on bail and Court must be satisfied, that the Accused was not guilty of such offence, and that he did not commit any offence while on bail.

Hon'ble Apex Court Held, while disposing of appeal: (i) Grant of bail would depend upon a circumstance which had nothing to do with the offence of money laundering. On this ground alone, Section 45 would have to be struck down as being manifestly arbitrary and providing a procedure which is not fair or just and would, thus, violate both Articles 14 and 21 of Constitution.

(ii) Another interesting feature of Section 45 was that, twin conditions that need to be satisfied under said Section were that there were reasonable grounds for believing that, accused was not guilty of "such offence" and that he was not likely to commit any offence while on bail. Expression "such offence" would be relatable only to an offence in Part A of Schedule. Thus, in an application made for bail, where offence of money laundering was involved, if Section 45 was to be applied, Court must be satisfied that, there were reasonable grounds for believing that, he was not guilty of the offence under Part A of Schedule, which was not offence of money laundering, but which was a completely different offence. Twin conditions laid down in Section 45 would have no nexus whatsoever with a bail application which concerned itself with offence of money laundering, for if Section 45 was to apply, Court did not apply its mind to whether person prosecuted was guilty of offence of money laundering, but instead applied its mind to whether such person is guilty of scheduled or predicate offence. Bail would be denied on grounds germane to scheduled or predicate offence, whereas person prosecuted would ultimately be punished for a completely different offence- namely, money laundering. This, again, was laying down of a condition which had no nexus with the offence of money laundering at all, and a person who might prove that there were reasonable grounds for believing that, he was not guilty of offence of money laundering might yet be denied bail, because he was unable to prove that, there were reasonable grounds for believing that he was not guilty of scheduled or predicate offence. This would again lead to a manifestly arbitrary, discriminatory and unjust result which would invalidate Section.

(iii) It could not be said that, Section 45 of the Act, imposed two conditions which were akin to conditions that were specified for grant of ordinary bail. It was obvious that, twin conditions set down in Section 45 of Act, were a much higher threshold bar. In fact, presumption of innocence, which was attached to any person being prosecuted of an offence, was inverted by conditions specified in Section 45 of Act, whereas for grant of ordinary bail, presumption of innocence attached. Under Section 45 of Act, Court must be satisfied that, there were reasonable grounds to believe that, person was not guilty of such offence and that he was not likely to commit any offence while on bail.

(iv) Section 45 of Act, was a drastic provision which turns on its head presumption of innocence which was fundamental to a person accused of any offence. Before application of a Section which made drastic inroads into fundamental right of personal liberty guaranteed by Article 21 of Constitution of India, it must be sure that, such provision furthered a compelling State interest for tackling serious crime. Absent any such compelling State interest, indiscriminate application of provisions of Section 45 of Act would certainly violate Article 21 of Constitution. Provisions akin to Section 45 of Act had only been upheld on ground that, there was a compelling State interest in tackling crimes of an extremely heinous nature.

VI

J. Sekar Vs. Directorate of Enforcement, 2022

Hon'ble Judges/Coram: Vineet Saran and J.K. Maheshwari, JJ.

Act/ Sections: Section 120-B read with Section 409, 420 of Indian Penal Code, 1860 (IPC) - Section 13(2), read with Section 13(1)(c) and 13(1)(d) of the Prevention of Corruption Act, 1988 (PC Act) - Section 482 of the Code of Criminal Procedure, 1973 (CrPC) - Sections 3 and 4 of the Prevention of Money Laundering Act, 2002 (PMLA)

No. of pages of the original Judgement: 09

Citations: MANU/SC/0596/2022

Case Note: Criminal - Quashing of proceedings - Section 120-B read with Section 409, 420 of Indian Penal Code, 1860 (IPC) - Section 13(2), read with Section 13(1)(c) and 13(1)(d) of the Prevention of Corruption Act, 1988 (PC Act) - Section 482 of the Code of Criminal Procedure, 1973 (CrPC) - Sections 3 and 4 of the Prevention of Money Laundering Act, 2002 (PMLA) - High Court vide impugned judgment rejected the petition seeking quashing of proceedings - Hence the present appeal - Whether impugned judgment in view of the facts and circumstances of the case sustainable or liable to be set aside?

Facts: The present appeal was filed against the impugned judgment dismissing the petition filed for quashing of proceedings. The impugned judgment rejected Appellant's contention that FIR with respect to Schedule offence was closed for want of evidence and in absence of connected evidence with a crime of Schedule offence, prosecution for offences under Sections 3 & 4 of the PMLA unsustainable. It was also held that the offence of money laundering is independent of the Schedule offence because PMLA deals with the process or activity with respect to the proceeds of crime including concealment, possession, acquisition or use. However, in the light of the explanation of Section 44(1) of PMLA, the argument of the Appellant was repelled. Appellant, Managing Partner of a partnership firm engaged in sand mining was subjected to case registered by CBI for offences under Sections 120-B r/w 409, 420 of IPC and Section 13(2), r/w 13(1)(c) and 13(1)(d) of the PC Act against the Appellant and two others.

Hon'ble Apex Court Held, while allowing the Appeal: For proceeds of crime, as defined under Section 2(1)(u) of PMLA, the property seized would be relevant and its possession with recovery and claim thereto must be innocent. In the present case, the Schedule offence has not been made out because of lack of evidence. The Adjudicating Authority, at the time of refusing to continue the order of attachment under PMLA, was of the opinion that the record regarding banks and its officials who may be involved, is not on record. Therefore, for lack of identity of the source of collected money, it could not be reasonably believed by the Deputy Director (ED) that the unaccounted money is connected with the commission of offence under PMLA. Even in cases of PMLA, the Court cannot proceed on the basis of preponderance of probabilities. On perusal of the statement of Objects and Reasons specified in PMLA, it is the stringent law brought by Parliament to check money laundering. Thus, the allegation must be proved beyond reasonable doubt in the Court. Even otherwise, it is incumbent upon the Court to look into the allegation and the material collected in support thereto and to find out whether the prima facie offence is made out. Unless the allegations are substantiated by the authorities and proved against a person in the court of law, the person is innocent. Looking to the facts as discussed hereinabove and the ratio of the judgments of this Court in Radheshyam Kejriwal (supra) and Ashoo Surendranath Tewari (supra), the chance to prove the allegations even for the purpose of provisions of PMLA in the Court are bleak. Therefore, till the allegations are proved, the Appellant would be innocent. The High Court by the impugned order has recorded the finding without due consideration of the letter of the I.T. Department and other material in right perspective. Therefore, these findings of the High Court cannot be sustained.

Accordingly, appeal is allowed

● 21 ●

VII

Serious Fraud Investigation Office Vs. Nittin Johari and Ors., 2019

Hon'ble Judges/Coram: N.V. Ramana, Mohan M. Shantanagoudar and Ajay Rastogi, JJ.

Ac/t Sections: Code of Criminal Procedure, 1973 (CrPC) - Section 173, Code of Criminal Procedure, 1973 (CrPC) - Section 439; Companies Act, 2013 - Section 212, Companies Act, 2013 - Section 212(1), Companies Act, 2013 - Section 212(12), Companies Act, 2013 - Section 212(15), Companies Act, 2013 - Section 212(6), Companies Act, 2013 - Section 212(7), Companies Act, 2013 - Section 212(8), Companies Act, 2013 - Section 447; Constitution of India - Article 14, Constitution of India - Article 21; Indian Penal Code, 1860 (IPC); Maharashtra Control of Organised Crime Act, 1999 - Section 21(4); Narcotic Drugs and Psychotropic Substances Act, 1985 - Section 37(1); Prevention of Money-laundering Act, 2002 - Section 45

No. of pages of the original Judgement: 08

Citation: AIR2019SC4380, (2019)9SCC165, MANU/SC/1246/2019

Case Note: Criminal - Grant of bail - Validity of - Section 439 of Code of Criminal Procedure, 1973 - It was alleged that Respondent No. 1 played an active role in using fraudulent letters of credit to avail of credit from lender banks - Respondent No. 1 came to be arrested - Respondent No. 1 applied for regular bail under Section 439 of Code which was dismissed by Special Judge (Companies Act) - Bail Application was subsequently filed before High Court, which came to be allowed - Hence, present appeal - Whether impugned order of grant of bail warrant any interference.

Facts: It was alleged that Respondent No. 1 played an active role in using fraudulent letters of credit to avail of credit from lender banks, in inflating Stock-in-Transit figures to avail of greater Drawing Power from banks, and in manipulating statements of accounts and other financial statements of company in the garb of adopting the Indian Accounting Standards. Respondent No. 1 came to be arrested. Respondent No. 1 applied for regular bail under Section 439 of the Code of Criminal Procedure, 1973 which was dismissed by the Special Judge (Companies Act). Bail Application No. 1791/ 2019 was subsequently filed before the High Court, which came to be allowed.

Hon'ble Apex Court Held, while allowing the appeal: (i) It was apparent that the Special Court, while considering the bail applications filed by Respondent No. 1 both prior and subsequent to the filing of the Investigation Report and complaint, has attempted to account not only for the conditions laid down in Section 212(6) of the Companies Act, but also of the general principles governing the grant of bail.

(ii) The High Court in the impugned order has failed to apply even these general principles. The High Court, after referring to certain portions of the complaint to ascertain the alleged role of Respondent No. 1, came to the conclusion that the role attributed to him was merely that of colluding with the co-Accused promoters in the commission of the offence in question. The Court referred to the principles governing the grant of bail as laid down by this Court in Ranjit sing Brahmajeet singh Sharma v. State of Maharashtra, which discusses the effect of the twin mandatory conditions pertaining to the grant of bail for offences under the Maharashtra Control of Organised Crime Act, 1999 as laid down in Section 21(4) thereof, similar to the conditions embodied in Section 212(6)(ii) of the Companies Act. However, the High Court went on to grant bail to Respondent No. 1 by observing that bail was justified on the broad probabilities of the case. This vague observation demonstrates non-application of mind on the part of the Court even under Section 439 of the Code of Criminal Procedure, even if keep aside the question of satisfaction of the mandatory requirements Under Section 212(6)(ii) of the Companies Act.

(iii) Therefore, the High Court had failed to apply its mind to all the circumstances that were required to be considered while granting bail, particularly in relation to economic offences. Accordingly, the impugned order was hereby set aside.

VIII

Pankaj Jain Vs. Union of India (UOI) and Ors., 2018

Citation: AIR2018SC1155, (2018)5SCC743, MANU/SC/0151/2018

Act/ Sections: Section 88 of Code of Criminal Procedure, 1973 (Code), Section 65Of Prevention of Money Laundering Act, 2002

No. of pages of the original Judgement: 11

Hon'ble Judges/Coram: A.K. Sikri and Ashok Bhushan, JJ.

Case Note: Criminal - Bail Application - Rejection - Section 88 of Code of Criminal Procedure, 1973 (Code) - Present appeal filed challenging vires of Section 88 of Code and for quashing High Court's order - Whether Court should release Appellant accepting bond under Section 88 of Code

Facts: First Information Report was lodged and a charge sheet was submitted against several accused including the Appellant. The Trial Court took cognizance summoning the accused for appearance. The Appellant filed an application for quashing the entire criminal proceeding. The application was finally disposed off with directions to appear and surrenders before the Court and applies for bail, and then his bail application was to be considered and decided. The Appellant surrenders but the other accused did not appear. The Appellants filed application to release him on bond which was rejected. Aggrieved by an appeal was preferred which was dismissed by the High Court. Hence, present appeal was made.

Hon'ble Apex Court Held, while disposing of appeal: (i) The present Court noted that Section 88 of the Code did not confer any right on any person, who is present in a Court. Discretionary power given to the Court is for the purpose and object of ensuring appearance of such person in that Court or to any other Court into which the case may be transferred for trial. Discretion given under Section 88 to the Court did not confer any right on a person, who is present in the Court rather it is the power given to the Court to facilitate his appearance, which clearly indicates that use of word 'may' is discretionary and it is for the Court to exercise its discretion when situation so demands. It was further relevant to note that the word used in Section 88 "any person" has to be given wide meaning, which may include persons, who are not even accused in a case and appeared as witnesses.

(ii) This Court on two earlier occasions had granted liberty to the Appellant to make an application for bail before the Trial Court, the Appellant did not file any application for bail before the Trial Court and had insisted on releasing him on acceptance of bond under Section 88 of Code. The present Court noted that the Trial Court is to first consider the prayer of grant of bail of the Appellant. Thus, when the Appellant files a bail application, the same shall be considered forthwith by Trial Court taking into consideration his claim of disability and other relevant grounds which are urged or may be urged by the Appellant before it.

IX

Central Bureau of Investigation Vs. V. Vijay Sai Reddy, 2013

Hon'ble Judges/Coram: P. Sathasivam and M.Y. Eqbal, JJ.

Act/ Sections: Code of Criminal Procedure, 1973 (CrPC) - Section 437; Code of Criminal Procedure, 1973 (CrPC) - Section 91; Indian Penal Code 1860, (IPC) - Section 120-B, Indian Penal Code 1860, (IPC) - Section 409; Indian Penal Code 1860, (IPC) - Section 420; Indian Penal Code 1860, (IPC) - Section 468; Indian Penal Code 1860, (IPC) - Section 471; Indian Penal Code 1860, (IPC) - Section 477A; Prevention Of Corruption Act, 1988 - Section 13(1)(c), Prevention Of Corruption Act, 1988 - Section 13(2), Prevention Of Corruption Act, 1988 - Section 9; Prevention Of Money-laundering Act, 2002 - Section 3

No. of pages of the Original Judgement: 08

Citation: AIR2013SC2216, (2013)7SCC452, MANU/SC/0486/2013

Case Note: Criminal - Grant of bail - Section 437 of Code of Criminal Procedure, 1973 - Special Judge granted bail to Accused for charges under Section 120-B, Section 409, Section 420 and 477A of IPC and Section 13(2), Section 13(1)(c) and Section 13(1)(d) of Act and same was affirmed by High Court. This Appeal Whether, High Court had mistakenly taken into account irrelevant materials and kept out relevant materials, which had to be considered for grant of bail - Held, cancellation of bail necessarily involves review of a decision already made, it should always be exercised very sparingly by Court of law without expressing any opinion on merits -

Thereby it was true that Special Judge while granting bail imposed certain conditions and High Court had also added some more additional conditions - However, taking note of few instances in which how Respondent had acted, it could not be possible for investigating agency to collect remaining materials for remaining three charge sheets to be filed - Further in such circumstances, Court was satisfied firstly Special Court took irrelevant materials for consideration for grant of bail and secondly, High Court had arrived definite conclusion that several findings of Special Court was unacceptable or irrelevant but ultimately affirmed order of special Judge granting bail - Moreover, during course of hearing, it was brought to Court notice that marriage of daughter of Respondent had been fixed for 26.05.2013 - Thus, taking note of said aspect, Court directed Respondent to surrender on or before 05.06.2013 before Special Court for being sent to custody. Hence, it was held that Special Judge committed an error in granting bail and same was erroneously affirmed by High Court - Therefore, Court set aside both orders of Special Judge and High Court granting bail to A-2 and allow appeal filed by CBI with a direction to complete all investigation relating to remaining three charge sheets and file appropriate report before trial Court within a period of four months - Appeal allowed.

Facts: V. Vijay Sai Reddy-the Respondent herein was named as an accused at Sl. No. 2 in the FIR dated 17.08.2011 (after the chargesheet was framed, he was arrayed as A-2 and hereinafter, he will be referred to as A-2). The Respondent herein was the founder Director of M/s. Jagathi Publications and was the Financial Advisor for the group of companies of Y.S. Jagan Mohan Reddy (A-1). He was arrested on 02.01.2012 and was in police custody from 04.01.2012 to 09.01.2012 and again from 11.01.2012 to 17.01.2012. On 27.01.2012, he filed an application for grant of regular bail Under Section 437 of the Code of Criminal Procedure, 1973 (in short 'the Code') before the Court of the Special Judge for CBI Cases at Hyderabad. The Special Judge, by order dated 21.03.2012, dismissed his application for bail.

Ratio Decidendi: "No order shall be passed without considering all aspects of matter."

౴

X

National Alliance for People's Movements and Ors. Vs. The State of Maharashtra and Ors., 2020

Citation: AIR2020SC4448, (2020)9SCC698, MANU/SC/0702/2020

Act/ Sections: offences under Special Acts such as MCOC, PMLA, MPID, NDPS, UAPA

No. of pages of the original Judgement: 06

Hon'ble Judges/Coram: S.A. Bobde, C.J.I., A.S. Bopanna and V. Ramasubramanian, JJ.

Case Note: Criminal - Release of prisoners - Unprecedented Circumstances due to Pandemic - High Powered Committee formed at state level to categorise temporary release - Petitioners sought clarifications and requested for exclusion of certain categories in the form of clarification - High Court vide impugned findings refused to interfere with the orders of High-Powered Committee - Hence, the present appeal

Facts: The Petitioners moved before High Court claiming to be in Public Interest seeking that the decision of the High Powered Committee ('HPC') dated 25.03.2020 to the extent of relevant clauses of HPC meeting dated

11.05.2020 excluding certain categories of offences as provided in relevant paragraphs for the purpose of grant of interim bail and corrigendum dated 18.05.2020 of the Minutes of the Meeting of HPC dated 11.05.2020 to the extent of clarification that the class and/or category of offences determined for temporary release be not read as a direction made by it for mandatory release of prisoners falling in that category and a further clarification that the case of every prisoner be considered on case to case basis for deciding the temporary release of such prisoners. The Petitioners also sought for a direction to the Respondents to release the prisoners convicted for life imprisonment without insisting that they were released in the past at least twice, either on furlough or parole. The High Court declined to interfere with decision of the HPC and hence the present petition.

Hon'ble Apex Court, Held, while dismissing the Appeals: The entire right to claim such interim bail has arisen in the unprecedented circumstance of the pandemic and the consideration for interim bail is not in the nature of a statutory right for bail based on other legal consideration but is more in the nature of human right to safeguard the health. The provision for bail as otherwise provided in law in any case would be considered by the competent courts if such right for bail is made out before the competent court irrespective of the pandemic or not. The present option provided is only as a solution to help decongestion and to avoid the spread of virus.

The very purpose of directing each of the States/Union Territories to constitute a High-Powered Committee is that the HPC taking note of the subsisting position in such State will take a decision in the matter as the HPC will have the wherewithal to secure all details and take a decision. If the said aspect is kept in view, it is noticed that by the guideline

dated 25.03.2020 the Committee in question has categorised the undertrials/convicted persons by the nature of the crime and the length of the punishment which will take care of the severity in the process of consideration. In that regard, insofar as the undertrial/convicted persons charged under the common law, namely, the Indian Penal Code; they are classified into two categories i.e., category-(i) as punishment below 7 years and category-(ii) as punishment above 7 years so that the consideration could be in that manner. The Committee has thought it fit to separately classify the undertrials/convicted persons who are charged under the Special Enactments irrespective of the duration of imprisonment notwithstanding the fact that the punishment imposed could be less than

7 years. In that regard, what has weighed with the HPC is that such enactments provide for additional restrictions on grant of bail in addition to those under the Code of Criminal Procedure. The said categorisation cannot be considered as unreasonable since at the first instance, based on the categorisation made a consideration is required by the Court for grant of interim bail if such undertrial/convicted person is seeking bail purely on taking benefit of the notification issued pursuant to such decision taken by the HPC. The exclusion made has a reasonable basis and cannot be termed arbitrary.

Having stated so it is necessary to indicate that the cause for grievance may arise for an individual undertrial/convicted prisoner only if such person has been discriminated as against the prisoner in the same category for which the benefit has been provided by the categorization made by the HPC. That apart the intention being to decongest the prisons, as a first step the release of the prisoners based on the impugned guidelines, held to be unflawed would be made. If, despite the release of the undertrial/convicted prisoners in the categories presently made does not achieve the purpose and the fact that additional prisons are set up also does not suffice and, in that context, if any modification with regard to the categories made by HPC is necessary; certainly, it would be open for the HPC to take note of the same and apply their mind to modify its guidelines in that regard.

Therefore, it would still be open for the Petitioners to obtain necessary statistics and if any modification of the guidelines is necessary in future, they will be at liberty to submit an appropriate representation to the HPC which would in that circumstance look into the same and arrive at a conclusion at its discretion depending on the need or otherwise to modify its guidelines. With the afore-stated observations, the above petition was dismissed. Decided On: 13.07.2017

XI

Girish Kumar Suneja Vs. C.B.I., 2017

Hon'ble Judges/Coram: Madan B. Lokur, Kurian Joseph and A.K. Sikri, JJ.

Act/ Sections: NDIAN PENAL CODE, 1860 (IPC) - Section 120B; INDIAN PENAL CODE, 1860 (IPC) - Section 409; INDIAN PENAL CODE, 1860 (IPC) - Section 420; PREVENTION OF CORRUPTION ACT, 1988 - Section 13(1)(C); PREVENTION OF CORRUPTION ACT, 1988 - Section 13(1)(D); CODE OF CRIMINAL PROCEDURE, 1973 (CrPC) - Section 397, Prevention of Money-Laundering Act, 2002 and other allied offences.

No. of pages of the Original Judgement: 022

Citation: AIR2017SC3620, (2017)14SCC809,MANU/SC/0829/2017

Case Note: Criminal - Coal block allocation - Impeding progress in investigation - Jurisdiction of Court - Sections 120B, 409, 420 of Indian Penal Code, 1860, Sections 13(1)(c) and 13(1)(d) of Prevention of Corruption Act, 1988 and Section 397 of Code of Criminal Procedure, 1973 - Order of Trial Court that no other Court was entitled to entertain any prayer made for stay or impeding progress in investigation or trial of coal block allocation cases was confirmed by High Court - Hence, present appeal by Appellants - Whether order whereby any request for stay or impeding progress in investigation or trial of coal block allocation cases made only to Trial Court and no other Court was maintainable.

Facts: Case was registered under Sections 120B, 409, 420 of the Indian Penal Code and Section 13(1)(c) and Section 13(1)(d) of the Prevention of Corruption Act against Appellant arising out of the illegal allocation of coal blocks. Trial Court passed order that no other Court was entitled to entertain any prayer made for stay or impeding the progress in the investigation or the trial of the coal block allocation cases. The High Court held that the petition should be dismissed on ground of non-maintainability. Hence, present appeal filed by Appellants.

Hon'ble Apex Court Held, while dismissing/allowing the appeal: (i) The entitlement of the Appellants to file a revision petition in the High Court was taken away and thereby the High Court was deprived of exercising its extraordinary discretionary power available under Section 397 of the Code of Criminal Procedure.

(ii) The coal block allocation cases were distinct from other cases since they had a massive impact on public interest and there had been large scale illegalities associated with the allocation of coal blocks. It was therefore necessary to treat these cases differentially since they form a unique identifiable category. Treating the entire batch of coal block allocation cases in a particular manner different from the usual cases was not a violation of Articles of the Constitution.

(iii) The width and ambit of the investigation and larger public interest was considered and order was passed reserving the right of the Accused to move to Present Court if there was a grievance against the order passed by the Trial Court during the trial and that this would ensure that progress in the trial was not hampered.

XII

Center for PIL and Ors. Vs. Union of India (UOI) and Ors., 2011

Hon'ble Judges/Coram: G.S. Singhvi and A.K. Ganguly, JJ.

Act/ Sections: Code of Criminal Procedure, 1973 (CrPC) - Section 24; Code of Criminal Procedure, 1973 (CrPC) - Section 46; Delhi Special Police Establishment Act, 1946 - Section 5; Prevention of Money-Laundering Act, 2002 - Section 46

No. of the pages of the Original Judgement: 07

Citation: (2012)3SCC117, MANU/SC/0542/2011

Case Note: Criminal - Appointment of Special Public Prosecutor - Section 46 of the Prevention of Money Laundering Act 2002; Section 24 of the Criminal Procedure Code, 1973 (Cr.P.C) - Whether appointment of lawyers in present case is prerogative of Government - Held, normally Central or State Government, make such appointments - However, having regard to larger issue of public interest involved in proper investigation of case and ultimate unearthing of crime, Court requested senior counsel for Central Bureau of Investigation (CBI) and Enforcement Directorate (ED), to suggest names of advocates who could undertake responsibility of conducting prosecution as Special Public Prosecutor in 2G Spectrum case - Expression "prerogative" cannot be used in context of statutory provision - Under Constitutional and statutory framework, nothing is known as prerogative - Expression "person conducting the prosecution before the Special Court" in Section 46(1) means that such person must either be appointed by Central or State Government after following procedure prescribed in Sub-Section (4), (5) along with Sub-Section (7) of Section 24 Cr.P.C or in alternative after following procedure in Section 24(6) or (7) of Code - Expression 'under' occurring in Section 46(2) must be construed in manner consistent with dignity of office of Public Prosecutor - Special Public Prosecutor cannot be treated as Government employee but may be lawyer on Government panel - In interest of fair prosecution of case, Mr. U.U. Lalit suitably appointed as Special Public Prosecutor to conduct prosecution on behalf of CBI and ED and he may choose two advocates on panel of CBI to assist him.

Facts: In view of those peculiar facts of this case, and various orders passed by it from time to time, this Court is of the opinion that in the matter of appointment of the Special Public Prosecutor, utmost fairness and objectivity should be observed. It is beyond dispute that for a successful prosecution, the appointment of a very competent Special Public Prosecutor is of the essence. This Court is aware of the fact that normally, in matter of appointment of a Special Public Prosecutor, the Central Government or State Government, as the case may be, make such appointments. Since the Court is monitoring the case and it is of the view that a competent prosecution is of utmost importance, having regard to the demands of public interest, this Court requested Mr. K.K. Venugopal, learned senior counsel for CBI and ED, to suggest certain names of learned advocates who can undertake the responsibility of conducting the prosecution as a Special Public Prosecutor in the case.

Ratio Decidendi: "Only Supreme Court shall have power to appoint Special Public Prosecutor as empowered by law."

XIII

Union of India (UOI) Vs. Varinder Singh and Ors., 2017

Hon'ble Judges/Coram: Arun Mishra and Amitava Roy, JJ.

Act/ Sections: PREVENTION OF MONEY-LAUNDERING ACT, 2002 – Section 45

No. of pages of the original Judgement: 03

Citation: (2018)15SCC248, MANU/SC/1227/2017

Case Note: The High Court has not complied with the requirement of Section 45 of the Prevention of Money Laundering Act, 2002. While granting bail, the High Court has failed to comply with the requirement of condition (ii) of Section 45 of the PMLA. This Court in Gautam Kundu v. Directorate of Enforcement (Prevention of Money Laundering Act), Government of India through Manoj Kumar, Assistant Director, Eastern Region Recent Apex Judgments (R.A.J.) 622 : (2015) 16 SCC 1 has laid down thus: The learned Solicitor General submitted that Section 45 of PMLA refers only to the term "Special Court" and therefore has to be given restricted meaning. According to him, PMLA is a "Special Law" applicable to the subject of money-laundering, and deals with economic offenders and white-collar criminals. Section 45 of PMLA makes the offence of money laundering cognizable and non-bailable and also provides that notwithstanding the provisions of Criminal Procedure Code, 1973, no person accused of an offence punishable for a term of imprisonment of more than three years under Part A of the Schedule shall be released on bail or on his own bond, unless the Public Prosecutor has been given an opportunity to oppose the application for such release.

Facts: The complaint is filed against the Appellant on the allegations of committing the offence punishable Under Section 4 of PMLA. The contention raised on behalf of the Appellant that no offence Under Section 24 of the SEBI Act is made out against the Appellant, which is a scheduled offence under PMLA, needs to be considered from the materials collected during the investigation by the Respondents. There is no order as yet passed by a competent court of law, holding that no offence is made out against the Appellant Under Section 24 of the SEBI Act and it would be noteworthy that a criminal revision praying for quashing the proceedings initiated against the Appellant Under Section 24 of the SEBI Act is still pending for hearing before the High Court. We have noted that Section 45 of PMLA will have overriding effect on the general provisions of the Code of Criminal Procedure in case of conflict between them. As mentioned earlier, Section 45 of PMLA imposes two conditions for grant of bail, specified under the said Act. We have not missed the proviso to Section 45 of the said Act which indicates that the legislature has carved out an exception for grant of bail by a Special Court when any person is under the age of 16 years or is a woman or is a sick or infirm. Therefore, there is no doubt that the conditions laid down Under Section 45A of PMLA, would bind the High Court as the provisions of special law having overriding effect on the provisions of Section 439 of the Code of Criminal Procedure for grant of bail to any person accused of committing offence punishable Under Section 4 of PMLA, even when the application for bail is considered Under Section 439 of the Code of Criminal Procedure."

It is the case where the Appellant is not only involved in the PMLA but also in the Narcotic Drugs and Psychotropic Substances Act, 1985 (in short 'the NDPS Act'). Without complying with the requirements of Section 45 of the PMLA, the High Court should not have granted the bail. As such the impugned order is set aside. The Respondents be arrested forthwith.

Hon'ble Apex Court Held, while allowing the appeal: Section 45 of the PMLA starts with a non obstante clause which indicates that the provisions laid down in Section 45 of PMLA will have overriding effect on the general provisions of the Code of Criminal Procedure in case of conflict between them. Section 45 of PMLA imposes the following two conditions for grant of bail to any person accused of an offence punishable for a term of imprisonment of more than three years under Part-A of the Schedule to PMLA:(i) That the prosecutor must be given an opportunity to oppose the application for bail; and

(ii) That the Court must be satisfied that there are reasonable grounds for believing that the accused person is not guilty of such offence and that he is not likely to commit any offence while on bail.

The appeal is allowed.

XIV

Vijay Narendra Kumar Kothari Vs. Directorate of Enforcement

Hon'ble Judges/Coram: U.U. Lalit and Ajay Rastogi, JJ.

Act/ Sections: Prevention of Money Laundering Act, 2002 - Section 3, Prevention of Money Laundering Act, 2002 - Section 4, Prevention of Money Laundering Act, 2002 - Section 45

No. of pages of the Original Judgement: 03

Citations: MANU/SC/0773/2021

Case Note: The Appellant along with two persons, namely, Anil Chokhara and Saurabh Pandit as well as three corporate entities, named, Yogeshwar Diamonds Pvt. Ltd., Shree Charbhuja Diamonds Pvt. Ltd., and, Kanika Gems Pvt. Ltd., are facing prosecution in Complaint Case No. 9/2017 in ECIR/ 05/MBZO/2016 in the Court of Sessions, City Civil and Sessions Court for Greater Bombay at Mumbai in respect of offences punishable Under Sections 3 and 4 of the Prevention of Money Laundering Act, 2002. One more person, namely, Sanjay Jain has since then been added as an Accused through supplementary charge-sheet vide Complaint Case No. 13/2017 in said ECIR Case.

Mr. Saurabh Kirpal, Learned Senior Advocate appearing in support of the appeal submits inter alia: (a) After due investigation, the draft charges have been filed by the Department, which is indicative of the fact that the investigation into the crime is complete. (b) All the assets of the Appellant stand attached as of now. (c) The co-accused Anil Chokhara, Saurabh Pandit and Sanjay Jain have been released on bail by the concerned Courts and those orders have not been called in question at any stage. (d) The offences which the Appellant is alleged to have committed carry maximum sentence of seven years, as against which the Appellant has already undergone actual custody of two years and four months. On the other hand, Mr. S.V. Raju, learned Additional Solicitor General appearing for the Department submits: (a) Though the complaint was filed on 17-6-2017 and various processes were issued for attendance and cooperation, those processes were completely disregarded; and the Appellant had to be declared a Proclaimed Offender on 12-2-2018. (b) The Appellant surrendered only on 15-3-2019 i.e. more than a year after he was declared to be a Proclaimed Offender. (c) The transactions in question involve transmission of more than Rs. 518 Crores to the alleged exporters from Hong Kong. The transmission of valuable foreign exchange did not result in any importation of goods which in turn could have provided impetus for various economic activities. Thus, the Appellant and his co-accused were guilty of illegal transfers of valuable foreign exchange. (d) The first bail application preferred by the Appellant was rejected on 29-11-2019, which order was never put in challenge. (e) The bail orders releasing three co-accused were passed even before 29-11-2019 and as such, there is no change in the circumstances on that count. (f) The rigor of Section 45 would apply as the relevant provision was amended after the decision of this Court in Nikesh Tarachand Shah.

Without going into the question whether the rigor of Section 45 of the Act would still apply as a result of the amendment, in our view, the Appellant is entitled to the benefit of bail principally for the reasons:

(a) The length of custody undergone by the Appellant as against the maximum sentence that could be visited upon the Appellant under the offences in question.

(b) The fact that the investigation in the matter is complete and draft charges have been circulated.

(c) All other three co-accused have been released on bail.

In the circumstances, we direct as under:

(I) Subject to the Appellant furnishing cash security in the sum of Rs. 25,00,000/- (Rupees Twenty-Five Lakhs only) with two like sureties to the satisfaction of the Trial Court, the Appellant shall be released on bail, subject to such conditions as the Trial Court may deem appropriate to impose. Such conditions shall include:

(i) The Appellant shall remain present on every hearing before the concerned Court.

(ii) The Appellant shall not leave the City of Mumbai without express permission of the Trial Court.

(iii) The Appellant shall record his presence in the office of the Respondent No. 1 at Mumbai-400001 once in a month.

(iv) The Appellant shall not in any way misuse his liberty and influence any of the witnesses.

(II) In order to facilitate the exercise, the Appellant shall be produced before the concerned Court within three days from today and the exercise of assessing the validity and correctness of the sureties shall be completed within seven days.

With the aforesaid observations, the appeal stands allowed.

XV

N. Kannadasan and Ors. Vs. Ajoy Khose and Ors., 2009

Hon'ble Judges/Coram: S.B. Sinha and Mukundakam Sharma, JJ.

Act/ Sections: CONSUMER PROTECTION ACT, 1986 [REPEALED] - Section 6; Indian Electricity Act, 1910 [Repealed] - Section 4, Indian Electricity Act, 1910 [Repealed] - Section 4(1); City of Nagpur Corporation Act, 1948 - Section 15, Prevention of Money Laundering Act, 2002.

No. of pages of the Original Judgement: 37

Citation: (2009)7SCC1, [2009]7SCR668, MANU/SC/0926/2009

Case Note: Consumer - Eligibility - Justiciability of the recommendations of the Chief Justice for appointment of the Appellant as the President of the State Consumer Disputes Redressal Commission in terms of Section 16 of the Consumers Protection Act, 1986 was the question involved in the appeal

Facts: The appellant was an Advocate practicing in the Madras High Court. He was appointed as an Additional Judge of the said Court for a period of two years on or about 6th November, 2003. During his tenure as an Additional Judge a representation was made from the Members of the Bar alleging lack of probity against him inter alia contending: (A) (i) several orders had been passed by him granting bail in Narcotic Drugs and Psychotropic Substances (NDPS) matters in contravention of the mandate laid down in Section 37 of the NDPS Act despite the refusal of bail on earlier occasions either by him or by other Judges ;

(ii) bail granted by him had subsequently been cancelled by other Judges ;

(iii) Abuse of office to work the judicial system to his own benefit through his former juniors

(B) Adverse reports from intelligence agencies.

Indisputably he was not appointed as a Permanent Judge as a result whereof demitted his office on 5th November, 2005. He resumed practice in Madras High Court. On a query made by the High Court as to whether the appellant was entitled to pensionary and other benefits, the Government of India by its letter dated 29th March, 2007 replied that he be treated at par with the retired Judges of the High Court for the purposes of obtaining medical benefits but would not be entitled to any pensionary benefits.

In the meantime, on or about 6th November, 2006 he was appointed as an Additional Advocate General of the State of Madras. Appellant intended to have his name included in the list of retired Judges wherefore he wrote a letter to the Registrar General of the Madras High Court on 24th May, 2008. Indisputably his name was included in the said list by a Resolution adopted in that behalf by the Full Court on 11th July, 2008

Held, Appointment to the post of President of a State Commission must satisfy not only the eligibility criteria of the candidate but also undertaking of the process of consultation - For appointment as President of the State Commission, the Chief Justice of the High Court shall have the primacy and thus the term 'consultation' even for the said purpose shall mean 'concurrence' only - Constitutional scheme of independence of the judiciary embodied in Article 50 of the Constitution of India should not be eroded - Appeal dismissed.

XVI

Loop Telecom and Trading Limited Vs. Union of India (UOI) and Ors., 2022

Hon'ble Judges/Coram: Dr. D.Y. Chandrachud, Surya Kant and Vikram Nath, JJ.

Act/ Sections: Code of Civil Procedure, 1908 (CPC) - Section 11; Constitution of India - Article 14, Constitution of India - Article 32, Constitution of India - Article 136; Consumer Protection Act, 1986 - Section 9; Government of India (Transaction of Business) Rules, 1961; Income Tax Act, 1961; Indian Contract Act, 1872 - Section 20, Indian Contract Act, 1872 - Section 23, Indian Contract Act, 1872 - Section 24, Indian Contract Act, 1872 - Section 56, Indian Contract Act, 1872 - Section 65, Indian Contract Act, 1872 - Section 66; Indian Penal Code, 1860 (IPC) - Section 120B, Indian Penal Code, 1860 (IPC) - Section 420; Indian Telegraph Act, 1885 - Section 4, Indian Telegraph Act, 1885 - Section 4(1), Indian Telegraph Act, 1885 - Section 7B(1); Indian Trusts Act, 1882 - Section 84; Monopolies And Restrictive Trade Practices Act, 1969 - Section 5(1); Prevention of Corruption Act, 1988; Prevention of Money Laundering Act, 2002; Telecom Regulatory Authority of India (Amendment) Act, 2000; Telecom Regulatory Authority Of India Act, 1997 - Section 14, Telecom Regulatory Authority Of India Act, 1997 - Section 14(a), Telecom Regulatory Authority Of India Act, 1997 - Section 14A,

Telecom Regulatory Authority Of India Act, 1997 - Section 14A(7), Telecom Regulatory Authority Of India Act, 1997 - Section 14(1), Telecom Regulatory Authority Of India Act, 1997 - Section 14(2), Telecom Regulatory Authority Of India Act, 1997 - Section 15, Telecom Regulatory Authority Of India Act, 1997 - Section 16, Telecom Regulatory Authority Of India Act, 1997 - Section 18

No. of pages of the Original Judgement: 30

Citation: AIR2022SC1441, (2022)6SCC762, MANU/SC/0267/2022

Case Note: Media and Communication - Entry Fee - Refund - Unified Access Service Licences (UASL) - Twenty One Service Areas -Appellant claimed entitled to refund based on civil, contractual and constitutional principles - Appellant as contended prevented from providing services under the licences since Respondent's "First Come First Serve" policy was flawed, arbitrary and illegal - Licenses were accordingly quashed which caused frustration of each licence in the nature of a contract - Whether Appellant on such claims entitled to be claim as sought?

Facts: The Appellant claimed a refund of Entry Fee (together with interest) paid by it for 2G licences for twenty-one service areas. Earlier by the judgment of Apex Court in Centre for Public Interest Litigation v. Union of India, the 2G licences granted by the Union of India, including to the Appellant, were quashed. The Appellant claimed to be entitled to the refund of its Entry Fee.

Hon'ble Apex Court Held, while dismissing the Appeal: The beneficiaries of the patently unconstitutional mechanism deployed for the allocation of spectrum were corporate entities who were favoured under the "First Come First Serve" policy. The Appellant is one of them.

TDSAT has correctly come to the conclusion that the claim by the Appellant for refund of the Entry Fee could not have been entertained.

The Appellant has been the beneficiary of a manifestly arbitrary policy which was adopted by the Union government and which was quashed in the decision of this Court in CPIL (supra). That being the position, the Appellant would not be entitled to a refund of the Entry Fee even on the principle of restitution embodied in Section 65 of the Indian Contract Act.

Appellant was in pari delicto with DoT and the then officials of the Union government. The Appellant was the beneficiary of the "First Come First Serve" policy which was intended to favour a group of private bidding entities at the cost of the public exchequer. The contention of the Appellant that it was exculpated from any wrong doing by the judgment of this Court in CPIL (supra) is patently erroneous. The process leading up to the award of the UASLs and the allocation of the 2G spectrum was found to be arbitrary and constitutionally infirm.

No merit in the appeal and thus dismissed.

XVII

NKGSB Cooperative Bank Limited Vs. Subir Chakravarty and Ors., 2022

Hon'ble Judges/Coram: A.M. Khanwilkar and C.T. Ravikumar, JJ.

Act/ Sections: Prevention Of Money-laundering Act, 2002 - Section 17; Central Reserve Police Force Act 1949 - Section 2(g); Chemical Weapons Convention Act, 2000 - Section 22, Chemical Weapons Convention Act, 2000 - Section 23, Chemical Weapons Convention Act, 2000 - Section 24, Chemical Weapons Convention Act, 2000 - Section 37; Child And Adolescent Labour (prohibition And Regulation) Act, 1986 - Section 17A; Children Act, 1960 - Section 56; Code of Civil Procedure, 1908 (CPC) - Order XXVI Rule 17; Code of Criminal Procedure, 1973 (CrPC) - Section 12; Code of Criminal Procedure, 1973 (CrPC) - Section 154; Code of Criminal Procedure, 1973 (CrPC) - Section 165; Code of Criminal Procedure, 1973 (CrPC) - Section 17; Code of Criminal Procedure, 1973 (CrPC) - Section 284; Code of Criminal Procedure, 1973 (CrPC) - Section 34; Code of Criminal Procedure, 1973 (CrPC) - Section 55.

No. of pages of the Original Judgement: 21

Citation: AIR2022SC1325, MANU/SC/0247/2022

Case Note: Banking - Possession of Secured Assets and documents - Appointment of Advocate for such purpose - Section 14(1A) of the Securitization and Reconstruction of Financial Assets and Enforcement of

Security Interest Act, 2002 - Whether District Magistrate or the Chief Metropolitan Magistrate can appoint an advocate and authorize him/her to take possession as provided for in the statute?

Facts: The Bombay High Court vide its relevant judgment opined that the advocate, not being a subordinate officer to the CMM or DM, such appointment would be illegal. Against this decision, four separate appeals were filed by the concerned parties. On the other hand, the High Court of Madras took a contrary view that the advocate is regarded as an officer of the court and, thus, subordinate to the CMM or the DM. Against this decision, a special leave petition was filed by the borrowers. The High Courts of Kerala and Delhi have taken the same view. Hence the present appeals to adjudicate on whether Advocate can be appointment as one authorised to take possession of secured assets and connected document.

Hon'ble Apex Court Held, while disposing the Appeals: It is well established that an advocate is a guardian of constitutional morality and justice equally with the Judge. He has an important duty as that of a Judge. He bears responsibility towards the society and is expected to act with utmost sincerity and commitment to the cause of justice. He has a duty to the court first. As an officer of the court, he owes allegiance to a higher cause and cannot indulge in consciously misstating the facts or for that matter conceal any material fact within his knowledge.

There is no reason to assume that the advocate so appointed by the CMM/DM would misuse the task entrusted to him/her and that will not be carried out strictly as per law or it would be a case of abuse of power. Rather, going by the institutional faith or trust reposed on advocates being officers of the court, there must be a presumption that if an advocate is appointed as commissioner for execution of the orders passed by the CMM/DM under Section 14(1) of the 2002 Act, that responsibility and duty will be discharged honestly and in accordance with Rules of law.

A fortiori, the judgment and order of the Bombay High Court impugned in the present appeals is declared as not a good law. Whereas, the conclusion of the three High Courts namely, High Courts of Kerala, Madras and Delhi on the question under consideration upheld.

The appeals filed by the secured creditors are allowed. Resultantly, the impugned judgment and order passed by the Bombay High Court is set aside and the subject writ petition stands dismissed. The special leave petition filed by the borrowers against the impugned judgment and order of the Madras High Court is delinked for being heard for admission, on the limited issue regarding compliance or non-compliance of Clauses (i) to (ix) of Section 14 of the 2002 Act in the fact situation of the present case.

XVIII

Madras Bar Association Vs. Union of India (UOI) and Ors., 2021

Hon'ble Judges/Coram: L. Nageswara Rao, Hemant Gupta, and S. Ravindra Bhat, JJ.

Act/ Sections: Constitution Of India - Article 14; Constitution Of India - Article 21; Constitution Of India - Article 50; Industrial Disputes Act, 1947; Kerala Irrigation and Water Conservation Act, 2003; Kerala Irrigation and Water Conservation (Amendment) Act, 2006; Prevention of Money-Laundering Act, 2002

No. of pages of the Original Judgement: 64

Citation: MANU/SC/0429/2021

Case Note: Constitution - Validity of Statute - Vires thereof - Sections 12 and 13 of the Tribunal Reforms (Rationalisation and Conditions of Service) Ordinance, 2021 and Sections 184 and 186(2) of the Finance Act, 2017 as amended by the Tribunal Reforms (Rationalisation and Conditions of Service) Ordinance, 2021 - Whether provisions ultra vires Articles 14, 21 and 50 of the Constitution of India inasmuch as violative of the principles of separation of powers and independence of judiciary?

Facts: The Tribunal Reforms (Rationalization and Conditions of Service) Bill, 2021 introduced in Lok Sabha on 13.02.2021 could not be taken up for consideration. Bill was proposed to streamline tribunals and sought to abolish certain tribunals and other authorities, which "only add to another additional layer of litigation" and were not beneficial for the public at large. Thereafter, the Tribunal Reforms (Rationalisation and Conditions of Service) Ordinance, 2021 (Ordinance) was promulgated on 04.04.2021. Chapter II thereof made amendments to the Finance Act, 2017. The dispute raised in this Writ Petition relates to the first proviso to Section 184(1) according to which a person below the age of 50 years would not be eligible for appointment as Chairperson or Member and also the second proviso, read with the third proviso, which stipulated that the allowances and benefits payable to Chairpersons and Members would be the same as a Central Government officer holding a post carrying the same pay as that of the Chairpersons and Members. Section 184(7) stipulated that the Selection Committee would recommend a panel of two names for appointment to the post of Chairperson or Member and the Central Government to take a decision preferably within three months from the date of the recommendation of the Committee, notwithstanding any judgment, order or decree of any Court. The said provision was assailed. Section 184(11) which shall be deemed to have been inserted with effect from 26.05.2017 provided that the term of office of the Chairperson and Member of a tribunal would be four years. The age of retirement of the Chairperson and Members is specified as 70 years and 67 years, respectively. If the term of office or the age of retirement specified in the order of appointment issued by the Central Government for those who have been appointed between 26.05.2017 and 04.04.2021 is greater than that specified in Section 184(11), the term of office or the age of retirement shall be as set out in the order of appointment, subject to a maximum term of office of five years. The validity of Section 184(11) also challenged in the Writ Petition.

Hon'ble Apex Court Held, while allowing the Petition:

L. Nageswara Rao, J. : The doctrine of separation of powers informs the Indian constitutional structure and is an essential constituent of Rule of law. In other words, the doctrine of separation of powers, though not expressly engrafted in the Constitution, its sweep, operation and visibility are apparent from the scheme of the Indian Constitution. The Constitution has made demarcation, without drawing formal lines between the three organs-- legislature, executive and judiciary. Separation of powers between three organs, the legislature, executive and judiciary, is also nothing but a consequence of principles of equality enshrined in Article 14 of the Constitution of India. Accordingly, breach of separation of judicial power may amount to negation of equality under Article 14. A legislation can be invalidated on the basis of breach of the separation of powers since such breach is negation of equality Under Article 14 of the Constitution. Equality, Rule of law, judicial review and separation of powers form parts of the basic structure of the Constitution. Each of these concepts are intimately connected. There can be no Rule of law, if there is no equality before the law. These would be meaningless if the violation was not subject to the judicial review. All these would be redundant if the legislative, executive and judicial powers are vested in one organ. Therefore, the duty to decide whether the limits have been transgressed has been placed on the judiciary. Though, there is no rigid separation of governmental powers between the executive, legislative and judiciary, it is clear from the above judicial pronouncements and literature that separation of powers forms part of the basic structure of the Constitution. Violation of separation of powers would result in infringement of Article 14 of the Constitution. A legislation can be declared as unconstitutional if it is in violation of the principle of separation of powers.

The fundamental right to equality before law and equal protection of laws guaranteed by Article 14 of the Constitution, clearly includes a right to have the person's rights adjudicated by a forum which exercises judicial power in an impartial and independent manner.

The constitutional mandate is that the legislature should adhere to the principles laid down in Part IV of the Constitution of India while enacting legislations. No provision shall be made in legislative acts which would have the tendency of making inroads into the judicial sphere. Any such encroachment by the legislature would amount to violating the principles of separation of powers, judicial independence and the Rule of law. Independence of courts from the executive and the legislature is fundamental to the Rule of law and one of the basic tenets of the Indian Constitution. Separation of powers between the three organs, i.e., the legislature, the executive and the judiciary, is a consequence of the principles of equality as enshrined in Article 14 of the Constitution. Any incursion into the judicial domain by the other two wings of the Government would, thus, be unconstitutional.

To conclude, the first proviso and the second proviso, read with the third proviso, to Section 184 overriding the judgment of this Court in MBA-III in respect of fixing 50 years as minimum age for appointment and payment of HRA, Section 184(7) relating to recommendation of two names for each post by the SCSC and further, requiring the decision to be taken by the

Government preferably within three months are declared to be unconstitutional. Section 184(11) prescribing tenure of four years is contrary to the principles of separation of powers, independence of judiciary, Rule of law and Article 14 of the Constitution of India. Though, we have upheld the proviso to Section 184(11), the appointments made to the CESTAT pursuant to the interim orders passed by this Court shall be governed by the relevant statute and the Rules framed thereunder that existed prior to 26.05.2017. We have already taken notice of the notification dated 30.06.21 by way of which Rule 15 of the 2020 Rules dealing with HRA has been amended in conformity with our directions in MBA-III.

The Petitioner continues its relentless struggle in its endeavour to make tribunals effective avenues of administration of justice. The endeavour of the Petitioner is to extricate the tribunals from the clutches of the executive in the interest of independence of judiciary. Security of tenure, adequate remuneration and other conditions of service are necessary to ensure that Members of tribunals would feel secure during their tenure. The judgment in MBA-III was passed after a detailed dialogue with the learned Attorney General. Existence of large number of vacancies of Members and Chairpersons and the inordinate delay caused in filling them up has resulted in emasculation of the tribunals. The main reason for tribunalisation, which is to provide speedy justice, is not achieved as tribunals are wilting under the unbearable weight of the exploding docket. Undoubtedly, the legislature is free to exercise its power to make laws and the executive is the best judge to decide policy matters. However, it is high time that a serious effort is made by all concerned to ensure that all the vacancies in the tribunals are filled up without delay. Access to justice and confidence of the litigant public in impartial justice being administered by tribunals need to be restored.

The Writ Petition is disposed of accordingly.

Hemant Gupta, J. Therefore, in case of failing to secure reappointment, the candidate will not be able to resume practice is based upon apprehensions. Whether they are good or valid grounds to refuse reappointment can be subject matter of judicial review although I am of the opinion that the decision of the high-power Search and Selection Committee not to re-appoint a candidate may not warrant interference in exercise of judicial review.

Thus, first, second and third proviso to Section 184(1), the use of expression 'preferably' in Section 184(7) and the proviso to Section 184(11) are legal and valid as such provisions fall within the exclusive domain of the legislature. The legislature has not nullified the judgment of this Court on the above aspects as there were no such corresponding provisions in the 2020 Rules, which were part of judicial review process.

It is open to the legislature to fix tenure of the Chairperson and the members other than four years as the tenure of four years was found to be not tenable in MBA-III. Section 184(7) which contemplates that Select Committee should recommend a panel of two names is contrary to the directions of this Court in MBA-III. Thus, Section 184(11)(i) (ii) and Section 184(7) is declared to be void as the Ordinance has reiterated the provisions which were in 2020 Rules. The challenge to other provisions is not legally sustainable. The writ petition is thus dismissed except to the extent mentioned above.

S. Ravindra Bhat, J. : Accordingly, (i) The first proviso to Section 184(1) of the Finance Act, 2017, introduced by Section 12 of the Tribunals Reforms (Rationalisation and Conditions of Service) Ordinance, 2021 declared void and inoperative. Similarly, the second proviso to Section 184(1) of the Finance Act, 2017, introduced by Section 12 of the Tribunals Reforms (Rationalisation and Conditions of Service) Ordinance, 2021 held to be void and inoperative; (ii) Section 184(7) of the Finance Act, 2017, introduced by of the Finance Act, 2017 introduced by Section 12 of the Tribunals Reforms (Rationalisation and Conditions of Service) Ordinance, 2021 is hereby declared void and inoperative; (iii) Section 184(11)(i) and (ii) introduced by Section 12 of the Tribunals (Reforms Rationalisation and Conditions of Service) Ordinance, 2021 are hereby declared as void and unconstitutional; (iv) Consequently, the declaration of this Court in para 53(iv) of MBA-III shall prevail and the term of Chairperson of a Tribunal shall be five years or till she or he attains the age of 70 years, whichever is earlier and the term of Member of a Tribunal shall be five years or till she or he attains the age of 67 years, whichever is earlier.; (v) The retrospectivity given to the proviso to Section 184(11)-introduced by Section 12 of the Tribunals (Reforms Rationalisation and Conditions of Service) Ordinance, 2021 is hereby upheld; however, without in any manner affecting the appointments made to the post of Chairperson or members of various Tribunals, upto 04.04.2021. In other words, the retrospectivity of the provision shall not in any manner affect the tenures of the incumbents appointed as a consequence of this Court's various orders during the interregnum period; (vi) The writ petition is allowed to the above extent.

XIX

Rapid Metro Rail Gurgaon Limited and Ors. Vs. Haryana Mass Rapid Transport Corporation Limited and Ors., 2021

Hon'ble Judges/Coram: Dr. D.Y. Chandrachud, M.R. Shah and Sanjiv Khanna, JJ.

Act/ Sections: Arbitration And Conciliation Act, 1996 - Section 9, Arbitration And Conciliation Act, 1996 - Section 17; Companies Act, 1956; Companies Act, 2013 - Section 130, Companies Act, 2013 - Section 241(2), Companies Act, 2013 - Section 242; Constitution of India - Article 32, Constitution of India - Article 136, Constitution of India - Article 226; Prevention of Money Laundering Act, 2002; Specific Relief Act 1963 - Section 14

No. of pages of the Original Judgement: 32

Citation: MANU/SC/0223/2021

Case Note: Company - Debt due - Financial audit - Second Respondent entered into Concession Agreement with Appellant No. 1 for execution of

Project No. 1 on design, build, finance, operate and transfer basis - Respondent granted concession to appellant for period of ninety nine years - Respondent executed another Concession Agreement with appellant no.2 for execution of Project No. 2 - Appellants completed Projects, in meantime, all metro projects and projects would gave to first Respondent - Appellants issued notice of termination to second respondent seeking to bring end to Concession Agreement - Appellants wrote to second respondent intimating that divestment requirements contained in Concession Agreement had already been completed by it - However, second respondent had failed to fulfill its obligations to verify Appellants' compliance with such divestment requirements - NCLAT issued directions for entities, inasmuch as that they had to seek approval of former judge who was appointed to supervise resolution process, before alienating or creating third party rights on assets - Appellants presented memorandum to former judge to seek his approval for handover of Projects to respondents - Respondents issued notice of termination to appellants of Concession Agreement and directed appellants to handover Projects to respondent - Thereafter, former judge permitted appellants to handover possession and control of Projects to respondents - Respondents instituted Writ Petition before High Court challenging notice of termination issued by appellant - Directions were issued by Division Bench recording that consensus had been arrived at in presence of senior officers of contesting parties that Appellants decided to continue Operation and Maintenance of both metro lines - And, as far as debt due was concerned, direction was issued to Comptroller and Auditor General of India (CAG) to appoint team of auditors for financial audit of debt due - In pursuance of order of High Court, CAG filed Application, together with compliance affidavit, before High Court and report was submitted in sealed cover - CAG report adverts to scope of audit which was undertaken in respect of debt due under Concession Agreement - Respondents filed objections to audit report - Proceedings then came up before High Court, when on request of Petitioners before High Court, hearing was deferred - Hence, present appeal - Whether report of financial audit of debt due was complete and conclusive as per scope of audit as decided by CAG.

Facts: The second Respondent entered into a Concession Agreement with appellant no.1 for the execution of Project No. 1 on a design, build, finance, operate and transfer basis. Second Respondent granted a concession to appellant for a period of ninety nine years from the effective date, including the exclusive right, license and authority during the subsistence of the Concession Agreement to implement and operate Project No. 1. The second respondent issued another RFQ/RFP for developing a metro rail link for Project No. 2. The bid submitted by the consortium was accepted by second respondent, which issued a letter of award. Pursuant to the letter of award, the consortium promoted and incorporated the second Appellant which would fulfill the obligations and exercise the rights of the consortium under the letter of award. Thereafter, a Concession Agreement was entered into between second respondent and appellant no.2 for the execution of Project No. 2. The Appellants completed Projects and in the meantime, the Town and Country Planning Department of the Government directed that all metro projects and projects in the State would be handled by the first Respondent. The appellants issued a notice of termination to second respondent seeking to bring an end to the Concession Agreement. Further, the Appellants responded to the letter of second respondent complaining of material breaches alleged to have been committed by the Appellants under their respective Concession Agreements. The appellants wrote to second respondent intimating that the divestment requirements contained in the Concession Agreement had already been completed by it. However, second respondent had failed to fulfill its obligations to verify appellants's compliance with such divestment requirements. NCLAT issued directions for the entities which had been categorized in the red category, inasmuch as that they had to seek the approval of former judge who was appointed to supervise resolution process before alienating, encumbering, transferring or creating third party rights on assets. Appellants presented a memorandum to former judge to seek his approval for handover of the Projects. The Respondents issued a notice of termination under the Concession Agreement. Terminating the agreement, they directed appellants to handover Projects to first respondent. The former judge permitted appellants to handover possession and control of Projects pursuant to the termination of the Concession Agreement. The Respondents instituted a Writ Petition before the High Court challenging notice of termination issued by appellant, inter alia, on the ground that the period of ninety days shall start from the date of permission, which had not been yet granted by former judge. The directions were issued by the Division Bench recording that a consensus had been arrived at in the presence of senior officers of the contesting parties by which appellants had decided to continue the Operation and Maintenance of both the metro lines. As far as debt due as defined under the concession contract is concerned, direction was issued to the Comptroller and Auditor General of India (CAG) to appoint a team of auditors for the financial audit of the debt due and also for examining the scope of the audit of debt due audited by the second respondent with the assistance of the auditors appointed by the parties to the lis. The High Court allowed an extension of seven days for implementing the directions issued in its orders. In pursuance of the order of the High Court, the Comptroller and Auditor General of India, filed a Civil Miscellaneous Application, together with the compliance affidavit, before the High Court, stating that it had appointed a firm of chartered accountants, to undertake a financial audit of the debt due and sealed report was filed. Thereafter, an affidavit was filed before the High Court by the Advisor (Planning) on behalf of the Respondents, objecting to the audit report. The Division Bench of the High Court noted the affidavit that had been filed by the respondent no.1 and took the affidavit on record, while also noting the submission of appellants that the matter did not brook any delay. The hearing was then adjourned to facilitate filing of replies. The proceedings then came up before the High Court, when on the request of the counsel for the Petitioners before the High Court, the hearing was deferred.

Hon'ble Apex Court Held, while disposing off the appeal: (i) The course of events indicates that the entire order which was passed by the High Court was the outcome of sustained negotiations which took place between first and second appellant on the one hand, and respondents on the other, commencing from the invocation of the writ jurisdiction under Article 226. It was significant to note that recourse to the proceedings under Article 226 was taken by respondents, which challenged the termination notice and sought the continuation of the operation of the rapid metro lines which were under imminent threat of closure, once the notice period expired. The narration of events would make it abundantly clear that initially as a result of the order of stay granted by the High Court and thereafter consequent upon mutual discussions, appellants agreed to operate the rapid metro link Projects within which period the handover would take place. Equally, the concerns by appellants, as concessionaires, was that in terms of the Concession Agreements, eight per cent of the debt due had to be deposited in the Escrow Account in terms of the provisions contained in in Concession Agreement. All the parties specifically agreed before the High Court that there would be a reference to the CAG for conducting an audit for the purpose of determining the debt due. The High Court by its order, issued directions which were specifically noted to be emanating from the consensus arrived at in the presence of senior officers of both the parties.

(ii) The directions contained in the High Court's consent order makes it abundantly clear that the audit team appointed by CAG was to conduct a financial audit of the debt due and to examine the scope of the audit. The next important aspect of the consent order was the time bound process which was envisaged, with the audit being completed within thirty days and eighty per cent of the debt due being deposited within thirty days after the receipt of the audit report. The final aspect which needs to be emphasized was that the rest of the disputes between the parties arising out of the audit report were to be agitated in arbitration.

(iii) The order makes it abundantly clear that the basic purpose underlying the entrustment of the reference to the CAG was the determination of the debt due as defined under the Concession Contract. The High Court, it must be emphasized, was seized of a proceeding under Article 226 of the Constitution, and its writ jurisdiction had been invoked to challenge the notices of termination issued by appellants, and for ensuring that the consequence which would emanate on the expiry of the notice period of ninety days by the cessation of the metro operations could be prevented by the judicial intervention in the course of the public law jurisdiction. The issuance of a notice of termination, the consequences which would ensue, and the resolution of disputes was specifically provided in the arbitration agreement between the parties, which was an intrinsic part of the Concession Agreements. Hence, there was an evident interface between this element of public interest on the one hand and the contractual rights of the parties to the Concession Agreements on the other. However, when respondent moved the High Court under Article 226, they did so in view of the impending threat which was looming large on the horizon of the rapid metro operations being brought to a standstill as a result of the proximate expiry of the notice of ninety days preceding termination. The High Court was evidently concerned over a fundamental issue of public interest, which was the hardship that would be caused to commuters who use the rapid metro as a vehicle for mass transport. As such, the High Court's exercise of its writ jurisdiction under Article 226 in the present case was justified since non-interference, which would have inevitably led to the disruption of rapid metro lines, would have had disastrous consequences for the general public. However, as a measure of abundant caution, this court clarify that ordinarily the High Court in its jurisdiction under Article 226 would decline to entertain a dispute which was arbitrable. Moreover, remedies were available under the Arbitration and Conciliation Act, 1996 for seeking interim directions either under Section 9 before the Court vested with jurisdiction or under Section 17 before the Arbitral Tribunal itself.

(iv) It was also important to note that the termination of the Concession Agreements had consequences in terms of the provisions contained in the Agreement requiring a deposit of eighty per cent of the debt due. The contesting parties agreed to an independent third-party determination of this amount by a neutral entity, namely the CAG. The primary function of CAG was to appoint a team of auditors for conducting a financial audit of the debt due and in that process of also examine the scope of the audit. The orders issued by the High Court also envisaged that CAG would examine the scope of the audit. While the earlier order required CAG to examine the scope of the audit of the debt due suggested by second respondent, the subsequent order required the examination by CAG on the scope of the audit after bearing in mind the suggestions by both the parties in terms of the Concession Agreement. The expression in terms of the Concession Agreement indicates that the basis of the audit was to be what was envisaged in the Concession Agreements, which specifically defines the expression debt due. Pertinently, the original order specifies a strict time Schedule within which, on a determination being made by the auditor, eighty per cent of the debt due would be deposited by second respondent in the Escrow Account. This was however subject to the safeguard that it would be subject to any order that may be passed by NCLAT or by a competent statutory authority. However, it was further clarified that the rest of the disputes between the parties to the lis arising out of the audit report were to be agitated in arbitration proceedings.

(v) The underlying wrongdoing which was allegedly conducted by the promoters in the erstwhile management of company undoubtedly needs to be investigated. The process of pursuing the forensic audit, the investigation by the SFIO and by the law enforcement machinery must follow to its logical conclusion. The NCLT was supervising the resolution process with a government appointed Board now being in charge of the management. Equally, financing arrangements entered into by financial institutions towards fulfilling infrastructure projects, based on the sanctity of the commercial contracts, were to be duly observed. This facet had to be emphasized since it embodies a vital element of public interest as well. Commentators have noted that, deterioration in loan recovery not only leads to higher provisions and diminished profitability but also constrains banks lending capacity, thus affecting the economy adversely. Unless the dues which are assured to financial institutions as part of the arrangements which were envisaged in Concession Agreements were duly enforced, the structure of financing for infrastructure projects may well be in jeopardy. Such a consequence must be avoided by declining to accede to a request, such as that by respondents, which was to allow it to resile from its obligations. These obligations arise not only in terms of the Concession Agreements, but had been solemnly assumed before the High Court. Hence, on both counts, respondents could not be permitted to resile.

(vi) The intervention of this Court under Article 136 of the Constitution was sought having regard to the manner in which the proceedings before the High Court were being derailed. After respondent filed its affidavit, the High Court noted the Appellant's submission that the matter does not brook any delay" and yet adjourned the matter. Thereafter, when the proceedings came up, and the response filed by CAG was taken on the record, the hearing of the writ petitions was again deferred. This course of events indicates that the whole object and purpose behind setting down the timelines in the order stood the risk of being defeated. This Court had been constrained to intervene in the process in order to ensure that the sanctity of the understanding that was arrived at before the High Court was duly maintained. There was a vital public interest element in ensuring that monies which were liable to be deposited in the Escrow Account with a nationalised bank are duly deposited. Respondents, it must be emphasized, were not left without remedy. The deposit into the Escrow Account had to be maintained in that form and will abide by such orders that may be passed by NCLAT or by a competent statutory authority. Besides this, the Concession Agreements provides a clear-cut remedy for seeking reliefs under the arbitration agreement.

(vii) The invocation of the writ jurisdiction of the High Court under Article 226 of the Constitution by respondents was to challenge the termination notices and to obviate the consequence of the cessation of the rapid metro operations, which would have ensued on the expiry of the notice period. The arbitration Clause of the Concession Agreements provides sufficient recourse to remedies which can be availed of. That apart, the order of the High Court had also clarified that the rest of the dispute that remains after the deposit of eighty per cent of the debt due, either arising out of the CAG report, the validity of the termination notices issued by both the parties and any past or future inter se claims and liabilities shall be agitated and decided in the arbitration proceedings. In view of the order which this court propose to pass, the dispute between the High Court in the writ jurisdiction under Article 226 of the Constitution shall stand worked out by granting liberty to the parties to avail of their rights and remedies in accordance with law.

XX

National Spot Exchange Limited Vs. Anil Kohli, 2021

Hon'ble Judges/Coram: M.R. Shah and Aniruddha Bose, JJ.

Act/ Sections: Arbitration And Conciliation Act, 1996 - Section 34, Arbitration And Conciliation Act, 1996 - Section 34(3); Constitution of India - Article 142; Consumer Protection Act - Section 13(2); Electricity Act, 2003 - Section 125, Electricity Act, 2003 - Section 125(2), Forward Contracts (regulation) Act, 1952 - Section 27; Insolvency And Bankruptcy Code, 2016 - Section 7, Insolvency And Bankruptcy Code, 2016 - Section 61(1), Insolvency And Bankruptcy Code, 2016 - Section 61(2); Limitation Act, 1963 - Section 3, Limitation Act, 1963 - Section 4, Limitation Act, 1963 - Section 5, Limitation Act, 1963 - Section 12, Limitation Act, 1963 - Section 29(2); Limitation Act, 1963 - Schedule - Article 136; Maharashtra Protection of Depositors Act, 1999; Recovery Of Debts And Bankruptcy Insolvency Resolution And Bankruptcy Of Individuals And Partnership Firms Act, 1993 - Section 24, Recovery Of Debts And Bankruptcy Insolvency Resolution And Bankruptcy Of Individuals And Partnership Firms Act, 1993 - Section 31; Prevention of Money Laundering Act, 2002 - Section 50

No. of pages of the Original Judgement: 10

Citation: AIR2021SC4339, MANU/SC/0642/2021

Case Note: Insolvency - Rejection of Claim - Appeal filed against thereto dismissed as barred by time -Section 61(2) of the Insolvency and Bankruptcy

Code, 2016 (IBC) - Whether delay could be condoned beyond 30 days as prescribed?

Facts: In the instant appeal, National Company Law Appellate Tribunal, New Delhi (NCLAT) refused to condone the delay of 44 days in preferring the appeal against the order passed by the National Company Law Tribunal (NCLT), rejecting the claim of the Appellant herein. Hence, the present appeal was preferred.

Hon'ble Apex Court Held, while dismissing the Appeal: As per Section 61(2) of the IB Code, the appeal was required to be preferred within a period of thirty days. Therefore, the limitation period prescribed to prefer an appeal was 30 days. However, as per the proviso to Section 61(2) of the Code, the Appellate Tribunal may allow an appeal to be filed after the expiry of the said period of 30 days if it is satisfied that there was sufficient cause for not filing the appeal, but such period shall not exceed 15 days. Therefore, the Appellate Tribunal has no jurisdiction at all to condone the delay exceeding 15 days from the period of 30 days, as contemplated Under Section 61(2) of the IB Code.

Even the Appellant applied for the certified copy of the order passed by the adjudicating authority after a delay of 34 days. Therefore, even the certified copy of the order passed by the adjudicating authority was applied beyond the prescribed period of limitation, i.e., beyond 30 days.

No interference called for. The present appeal fails and deserves to be dismissed and is accordingly dismissed.

XXI

Subhash Kashinath Mahajan Vs. The State of Maharashtra and Ors. 2018

Hon'ble Judges/Coram: Adarsh Kumar Goel and U.U. Lalit, JJ.

Act/ Sections: Scheduled Castes and the Scheduled Tribes (Prevention of Atrocities) Act, 1989 - Section 3, Scheduled Castes and the Scheduled Tribes (Prevention of Atrocities) Act, 1989 - Section 3(1), Scheduled Castes and the Scheduled Tribes (Prevention of Atrocities) Act, 1989 - Section 3(1)(9), Scheduled Castes and the Scheduled Tribes (Prevention of Atrocities) Act, 1989 - Section 3(2), Scheduled Castes and the Scheduled Tribes (Prevention of Atrocities) Act, 1989 - Section 3(2)(7)(6), Scheduled Castes and the Scheduled Tribes (Prevention of Atrocities) Act, 1989 - Section 4, Scheduled Castes and the Scheduled Tribes (Prevention of Atrocities) Act, 1989 - Section 5, Scheduled Castes and the Scheduled Tribes (Prevention of Atrocities) Act, 1989 - Section 18, Scheduled Castes and the Scheduled Tribes (Prevention of Atrocities) Act, 1989 - Section 124A; Prevention of Money-Laundering Act, 2002 - Section 45; Sexual Harassment of Women at Workplace (Prevention, Prohibition and Redressal) Act, 2013

No. of pages of the Original Judgement: 34

Citation: AIR2018SC1498, (2018)6SCC454, MANU/SC/0275/2018

Case Note: Criminal - False Implication - Article 21 of Constitution of India - Present appeal filed against order wherein High Court rejected Appellants appeal of quashing proceedings against him - Whether directions be issued to protect fundamental right under Article 21 of Constitution against false implication and arrests.

Facts: The Appellant was serving as Director of Technical Education. The second Respondent was an employee of the department. Dr. Satish Bhise and Dr. Kishor Burade, who were his seniors made adverse entry in his annual confidential report that his integrity and character was not good. The second Respondent lodged FIR against the said two officers under the Atrocities Act. The Investigating Officer applied for sanction against them to the Director of Technical Education which was refused by the Appellant. Because of this, 'C' Summary Report was filed against Bhise and Burade which was not accepted by the Court. Aggrieved by a complainant was filed against the Appellant stating that he was not competent to grant/refuse sanction as the above two persons were Class-I officers and only the State Government could grant sanction. The Appellant filed a petition to the High Court for quashing the proceedings which was rejected. Hence, present appeal was filed.

Hon'ble Apex Court Held, while allowing appeal: (i) There could be no dispute with the proposition that mere unilateral allegation by any individual belonging to any caste, when such allegation was clearly motivated and false, could not be treated as enough to deprive a person of his liberty without an independent scrutiny. Thus, exclusion of provision for anticipatory bail could not possibly, by any reasonable interpretation, be treated as applicable when no case was made out or allegations were patently false or motivated. If this interpretation was not taken, it might be difficult for public servants to discharge their bona fide functions and, in given cases, they could be black mailed with the threat of a false case being registered under the Atrocities Act, without any protection of law. This could not be the scenario in a civilized society. Similarly, even a non-public servant could be black mailed to surrender his civil rights. This was not the intention of law. Such law could not stand judicial scrutiny. It would fall foul of guaranteed fundamental rights of fair and reasonable procedure being followed if a person was deprived of life and liberty.

(ii) Innocent citizens are termed as accused, which was not intended by the legislature. The legislature never intended to use the Atrocities Act as an instrument to blackmail or to wreak personal vengeance. The Act was also not intended to deter public servants from performing their bona fide duties. Thus, unless exclusion of anticipatory bail is limited to genuine cases and inapplicable to cases where there was no prima facie case was made out, there would be no protection available to innocent citizens. Thus, limiting the exclusion of anticipatory bail in such cases was essential for protection of fundamental right of life and liberty Under Article 21 of the Constitution.

(iii) The Present Court had no hesitation in holding that exclusion of provision for anticipatory bail would not apply when no prima facie case was made out or the case is patently false or mala fide. This may have to be determined by the Court concerned in facts and circumstances of each case in exercise of its judicial discretion. In doing so, the present Court was reiterating a well-established principle of law that protection of innocent against abuse of law is part of inherent jurisdiction of the Court being part of access to justice and protection of liberty against any oppressive action such as mala fide arrest.

(iv) The under privileged need to be protected against any atrocities to give effect to the Constitutional ideals. The Atrocities Act has been enacted with this objective. At the same time, the said Act cannot be converted into a charter for exploitation or oppression by any unscrupulous person or by police for extraneous reasons against other citizens as has been found on several occasions. Any harassment of an innocent citizen, irrespective of caste or religion, is against the guarantee of the Constitution. This Court must enforce such a guarantee. Law should not result in caste hatred. The preamble to the Constitution, which is the guiding star for interpretation, incorporates the values of liberty, equality and fraternity.

Adv. Jayprakash Somani's Videos On Law

1) SLP in Supreme Court / Special Leave Petitions in the Supreme Court of India

2) Transfer of Civil & Criminal Cases by the Supreme Court of India / Transfer of Matrimonial Cases

3) Appellate Jurisdiction of the Supreme Court of India

4) Jurisdictions of the Supreme Court of India

5) Public Interest Litigation in the Supreme Court of India / PIL in Supreme Court

6) Article 32 Writ Petitions in the Supreme Court of India

7) Bail Matters Top 10 Supreme Court Cases

8) FIR Quashing in High Court & Supreme Court

9) Bail & Anticipatory Bail Matters in Supreme Court

10) Insolvency & Bankruptcy Matters in the Supreme Court

11) Insolvency & Bankruptcy Code 2016 Part 1

12) Insolvency & Bankruptcy Code 2016 Part 2

13) Insolvency & Bankruptcy Code 2016 Part 3

14) Corporate Liquidation Process

15) Supreme Court Rules & Procedures Webinar of 2.5 hour on Zoom

16) RDDBFI Act, 1993 (Introduction)

17) The Indian Contact Act 1872

18) Negotiable Instruments Act (Introduction)

19) How to avoid matrimonial disputes& some more videos

20) SEBI Matters in the Supreme Court

21) Matrimonial Matters: Supreme Court's 20 Case Laws

22) Consumer Matters Supreme Court's 20 Case Laws

23) Service Matters Supreme Court's 20 Case Laws

24) How to Search Lawyer for Your Matter

25) Property Matters Supreme Court's 20 Case Laws

26) Bail Matters: Supreme Court's 20 Case Laws

27) Supreme Court / High Court Vacation Benches

28) 69000 Teacher's Recruitment Matters of UP Government in the Supreme Court

29) Contempt of Court Matters in the Supreme Court

30) Advocate Act's Matters in the Supreme Court

31) Business Law Matters in the Supreme Court

32) Banking Matters in the Supreme Court

33) Labour Law Matters in the Supreme Court

34) Arbitration Matters in the Supreme Court

35) Careers in Law -Zoom Webinar by Adv. Jayprakash Somani

36) Civil Matters in the Supreme Court

37) Consumer Protection Act | Consumer Matters in the Supreme Court

38) Corporate Matters in the Supreme Court

39) Criminal Matters in the Supreme Court

40) Role of Respondent in the Supreme Court of India

41) Motor Vehicle Accident Matters in Supreme Court with case laws

42) Article 131 Original Suits in Supreme Court

43) PIL in Supreme Court/ Public Interest Litigations in the Supreme Court of India'

44) CAB Citizenship Amendment Bill is not Unconstitutional

45) Supreme Court of India Cases & Process – Marathi

46) Legal Services Export / Export of Legal Services

47) Transfer of Matrimonial Cases by the Supreme Court of India

48) Public Interest Litigation PIL

49) The Specific Relief Act (Introduction)

50) Corporate Insolvency Resolution Process CIRP

51) ABMM's Career 5 - Careers in Law

52) Transfer of cases by Supreme Court

53) Writ Petitions in High Court & Supreme Court of India

54) Supreme Court Jurisdictions - Appeals, SLP, Writ Petitions, Transfer, Original, Review, Curative

55) LEGAL INDIA TV Show: Cases Handled in Supreme Court

56) Corporate Liquidation Process

57) Legal Services Export / Export of Legal Services

58) Corporate Laws

59) Election Matters- Supreme Court's 20 Case Laws

60) Companies Act, 2013

62) Competition Act, 2002

63) Banking Matters - Supreme Court's 20 Case Laws

64) Election Matters in the Supreme Court

65) Armed Forces Tribunal Matters in the Supreme Court

66) Compassionate Appointment Service matter

67) Foreign Exchange Management Act FEMA

68) Foreign Trade Policy 2021-26 Proposed

69) Customs Act 1962

70) Narcotic Drugs and Psychotropic Substances Act, 1985 NDPS Act

71) Foreign Trade Development & Regulation Act, 1992

72) How to Search Good Advocate in the Supreme Court of India

73) Sr. Adv Vikas Singh's Interview in Nani Palkhivala Wednesday Law Club

74) Indian Penal Code (I. P. C.)

75) Criminal Procedure Code (Cr. P. C.)

76) Commercial Courts & International Arbitration - by Mr. Jaideep Gupta, Senior Advocate in Nani Palkhivala Wednesday Law Club

77) Sr. Adv Ranji Thomos in Nani Palkhivala Wednesday Law Club

78) Urgent Matters in Supreme Court during vacations

79) 498A Bail Matters in Supreme Court

81) 376 Bail Matters in Supreme Court

82) 302, 304, 307, 308 Bail Matters in Supreme Court

83) 138, 420 Bail Matters in Supreme Court

84) POCSO Act Bail Matters in Supreme Court

85) NDPS Act Bail Matters in Supreme Court

86) What is ED (Enforcement Directorate)?

87) Prevention of Money Laundering Act, 2002 (PMLA Act)

88) Insolvency & Bankruptcy Code- Supreme Court Case Laws. Webinar in Nani Palkhivala Wednesday Law Club

89) What is NCLT & NCLAT?

90) Acquittal from 376- Supreme Court's some case laws in Nani Palkhivala Wednesday Law Club dt 28.7.22

91) Insolvency & Bankruptcy in India

92) Can we file case directly in the Supreme Court?

93) Adv. Anuja Pethia has cleared AOR Exam 2021 with 77% marks - Her interview in Nani Palkhivala Wednesday Law Club

94) Customs Act - Supreme Court Case Laws & Interview of AOR Adv. Anuja Pethia in Nani Palkhivala Law Club.

95) The Uttar Pradesh Public Service Tribunals Act, 1976

96) POCSO Act - Supreme Court Case Laws & Interview of AOR Adv. Shoumendu Mukharji & Adv. Nishant Verma in Nani Palkhivala Law Club.

97) Who Can Trigger CIRP Process Under Insolvency Law of India

98) The Uttar Pradesh Government Servant Discipline and Appeal Rules, 1999

99) CIRP Application Under Sec 7 by FC

100) Information Technology Act 2000

101) Uttar Pradesh Recruitment of Dependants of Government Servants Dying in Harness Rules, 1974

102) Foreign Exchange Management Act 1999 & Supreme Court's Case Laws on FEMA & Leading Case of AOR Exam in Nani Palkhivala Law Club.

103) Arbitration and Conciliation Act 1996 & It's Supreme Court Case Laws in Nani Palkhivala Wednesday Law Club.

104) Narcotic Drugs & Psychotropic Substances Act 1985 (NDPS Act) & It's Supreme Court Case Laws in Nani Palkhivala Wednesday Law Club.

105) Recovery of Debts and Bankruptcy Act 1993

106) Uttar Pradesh Land Revenue Code 2006

107) CIRP Application Under Sec 9 by OC

108) CIRP Application Under Sec 10 by CD

109) Hindu Succession Act, 1956

110) Maharashtra Civil Services Rules, 1981

111) Indian Contract Act, 1872 & Supreme Court's Case Laws" in Nani Palkhiwala Wednesday Law Club

112) Securities and Exchange Board of India Act, 1992 i. e. SEBI Act 1992 & Case Laws on Insiders Trading" in Nani Palkhiwala Wednesday Law Club

113) Moratorium Under Section 14 of IBC, 2016

114) Hindu Marriage Act, 1955

115) Maharashtra Land Revenue Code, 1966

116) 64 Leading Cases of AOR Exam Session 1 :- Cases 1 to16 in Nani Palkhiwala Wednesday Law Club

117) 64 Leading Cases of AOR Exam Session 2: Cases 17 to 32 in Nani Palkhivala Wednesday Law Club

118) 64 Leading Cases of AOR Examination Session 3: Cases 33 to 48 in Nani Palkhivala Wednesday Law Club

119) 64 Leading Cases of AOR Exam Session 4: Cases 49 to 64 in Nani Palkhivala Wednesday Law Club

List Of Adv. Jayprakash Somani's Published Books

1. Supreme Court of India's Leading Case Laws on 'Insolvency & Bankruptcy Code 2016'

2. Bail Matters – Supreme Court's Latest Leading Case Laws

3. Arbitration Matters- Supreme Court's Latest Leading Case Laws

4. Property Matters - Supreme Court's Latest Leading Case Laws

5. Matrimonial Matters- Supreme Court's Latest Leading Case Laws

6. Election Matters- Supreme Court's Latest Leading Case Laws

7.SEBI Matters- Supreme Court's Latest Leading Case Laws

8. Banking Matters- Supreme Court's Latest Leading Case Laws

9. Service Matters- Supreme Court's Latest Leading Case Laws

10. Contempt of Court Matters- Supreme Court's Latest Leading Case Laws

11. Consumer Protection Matters- Supreme Court's Latest Leading Case Laws

12. Corporate Law- Supreme Court's Latest Leading Case Laws

13. Supreme Court's AOR Exam- Leading Cases

14. Armed Force Tribunal - Supreme Court's Latest Leading Case Laws

15. Acquittal From 376 - Supreme Court's Latest Leading Case Laws

16. Negotiable instrument – Supreme Court's Latest Leading Case Laws

17. Contract Act- Supreme Court's Latest Leading Case Laws

18. Insider trading- Supreme Court's Latest Leading Case Laws

19. Foreign Exchange and Management Act- Supreme Court's Latest Leading Case Laws

20. Income Tax Act- Supreme Court's Latest Leading Case Laws

21. Company Law- Supreme Court's Latest Leading Case Laws

22. Competition & Monopoly Matters- Supreme Court's Latest Leading Case Laws

23. Compassionate Appointment- Service Matters- Supreme Court's Latest Leading Case Laws

24. Compulsory Retirement- Service Matters- Supreme Court's Latest Leading Case Laws

25. Voluntary Retirement- Service Matters- Supreme Court's Latest Leading Case Laws

26. Removal/Dismissal/Termination from Service- Supreme Court's Latest Leading Case Laws

27. Seniority- Service Matter- Supreme Court's Latest Leading Case Laws

28. Promotion- Service Matter- Supreme Court's Latest Leading Case Laws

29. Equal Pay for Equal Work- Service Matter- Supreme Court's Latest Leading Case Laws

30. Condition of Service- Service Matter- Supreme Court's Latest Leading Case Laws

31. Customs Act- Supreme Court's Leading Case Laws

32. Information Technology Act- Supreme Court's Leading Case Laws

33. SEC. 125 CR. P. C.- Supreme Court's Leading Case Laws

34. SEC. 498A OF I. P. C.- Supreme Court's Leading Case Laws

35. MOTOR VEHICLE ACT- Supreme Court's Leading Case Laws

36. CONDITION OF SERVICE- SERVICE MATTER- Supreme Court's Leading Case Laws

37. SUSPENSION- SERVICE MATTER- Supreme Court's Leading Case Laws

38. Reservation in SC, ST, OBC- Service Matter- Supreme Court's Leading Case Laws

39. NARCOTIC DRUGS AND PSYCHOTROPIC SUBSTANCES (NDPS) ACT - Supreme Court of India's Latest Leading Case Laws

40. SEC 302 IPC - Supreme Court of India's Latest Leading Case Laws

41. PROTECTION OF CHILDREN FROM SEXUAL OFFENCES ACT (POCSO) - Supreme Court of India's Latest Leading Case Laws

42. PMLA ACT BAIL MATTERS- Supreme Court of India's Leading Case Laws

Books are available online in India

1. Notion Press: https://notionpress.com/author/jayprakash_somani

2. Amazon: https://www.amazon.in/s?k=jayprakash+somani

3. Flipkart: https://www.flipkart.com/search?q=Jayprakash%20Somani

Books are available online at International Market

4. Amazon International: https://www.amazon.com/s?k=jayprakash+somani

5. Amazon United Kingdom: https://www.amazon.co.uk/s?k=jayprakash+somani

6. E-Books/Kindle edition at National & International Level: https://www.amazon.in/s?k=jaypraksh+somani